Signs from Heaven

Robbie Thomas

Copyright © 2006-2012 Robbie Thomas

Published by: Robbie Thomas Offices

ISBN-13: 978-1478193678

ISBN-10: 1478193670

Dedication

I dedicate this book to my best friend, who gave me life and taught me everything I am still to this day. All the moments we shared in life here have and will remain the most treasured memories. I will keep and take within my heart when we meet once again on the other side. There is nothing more beautiful than the love of a mother for her child. From this it gives me great perspective in my life to which I say to you: I can't love you any more than I do from the moment I opened my eyes and breathed the breath of life that you gave me. Precious is the time we spent together, just a reminder of what will be once more, for you are the love of my life; this I hold sacred always.

> My eyes open and gaze at wonder,
> Trapped between what is this I ponder,
> Seeing this angel before me as I stare,
> She gently whispers, "Baby, I am here,"
> Things start to ring in a rejoice,
>
> Nothing more beautiful than my mother's voice!

Thank you, Mother, for everything you are and have been for me; I love you dearly. Till we meet again someday...love you, Robbie

Acknowledgments

First and foremost I owe everything I am to my Lord and Savior Jesus Christ, for without the strength in which God gives me, the day in which I exist, I am nothing.... Thank You, God!

The love and compassion my "guides and angels" bring me in times of need and comfort. Showing me the proper guidance throughout my life. Will always treasure you forevermore.

To my family, I love you dearly. You are the inspiration behind much of what I do, you are the light in my life that keeps me grounded.

To Caroline Beagan, for writing that beautiful foreword for my book, your words are very moving and sure to capture many who read it. I thank you whole-heartedly; you are a beautiful individual!

To Debra Peden-Hughes, for the artwork for the book cover is priceless; your talent has exceeded my vision. Thank you! A true inspiration to draw from in the making of the very first thing people will see, thank you again!

To all the radio and television shows I have been on throughout the years along with the media coverage I have had, I thank you so very much!

To each and every individual whose life has changed by giving so much more meaning to themselves with the witnessing of miracles of spirit, may God bless you!

To all of you who are now reading *Signs from Heaven*, I hope it brings you peace and joy knowing within you are the tools of solace that will allow you to obtain the knowledge that the other side is but a whisper away.

God bless you all...Robbie.

Table of Contents

Foreword

Signs from Heaven is a book that will totally capture, entice and enlighten your mind body and soul. You are about to enter into a psychic journey that will captivate you beyond belief! I would ask of you, the reader, open your heart and mind in allowing the energy within to flow freely.

This book is a spiritual insight, from this world to our world beyond. You will feel inner warmth of all things spiritual. You will witness at first hand true genuine connections from all walks of life from our loved ones' souls that have crossed over from this life to the next, knowing that they are still with us and watching over us. While reading *Signs from Heaven*, you will discover that there are many ways in which a loved one can indeed come through to us, bringing us a sense of peace and harmony. Just to have the knowledge and understanding of life thereafter, knowing God is guiding us is the greatest gift of all.

Robbie gives us an in-depth description of how we can all have a greater understanding of the spirit world. Wrote from the heart, guided by God, Robbie has portrayed this book in a way that is sure to touch your hearts giving a true reflection. The gripping fortitude that is exemplified through the writings in this doctrine shine forth in the absolutely beautiful ways of expression not only showing us but to teach us how to look inward for key answers. From the moment the cover is turned open you will be entranced by the lessons of each aspect of the four cornerstones of spirituality, giving all who read it the sensational desire to read once more.

In this second book apart from his first book, *A Link to*

Heaven...Chats with the Other Side, Robbie writes an extraordinary spiritual trek that eventually leads him to move mountains. The unselfish journey Robbie undertakes to try and save a special angel in a far off land shows the will of spirit in the world around us. You become so attached to this heart-wrenching story that reveals the love of human kind it becomes a bitter sweet in the end of a journey with spirit.

Technology and the Internet has opened up a completely new and alternative gateway to our spiritual being, thus enabling us to communicate more efficiently with the other side. Robbie Thomas is our gateway on this side of our universe as a spirit messenger, for which I highly recommend you visit his site www.robbiethomas.net in complimenting your discovery. By taking hold of this vast array of literary directional love that was written for everyone to enhance his or her spiritual wellbeing, you are giving that spark of hope for your soul.

Caroline Beagan

Writer/Spiritualist

Introduction

We all feel we belong to the most inner spiritual source ever and this is true for we do come from and are a part of the greatest spirit of all, God. The quest for knowledge and/or feeling of goodness is a quest we all take in our lifetime to obtain the proper feeling of spirit in order to satisfy our inner self. Imagine a lifetime of searching and finding out you have it in you and it has been there all this time; what a relief it is to actually belong and be a part of a spiritual enlightenment. Taking the ever knowing of us and actually putting into practice the progressive steps to ensure this right of ours called spirit, we do undergo many trials and tribulations but all of those misconceptions are manmade that leave us thinking. We are and have been ordained with the spirit of God from the life on the other side to this life here and we carry every aspect of home, spirit, enlightenment and everything of good right in the depths of our hearts.

Findings ones way or searching is a trek in itself but the rewards are so satisfying leaving the absolute to anything missing actually found in spirit. Soul searching or finding spirituality is always and will be a part of everyone's life in this world; it's something that is in the heart of hearts…your soul! To actually elaborate on anything less is to say, *we have no hope or faith in anything whatsoever therefore we must evolve from dust and return to dust then just blow in the wind,* not much sense there now is there.

That deep feeling you feel when you are elated is exactly what comes from your inner feelings and your soul. It lends credence of all good and extends that openness that results in positiveness of everything enlightened you seek.

Inner signs of us are shown in each beautiful overwhelming feeling we have in the light of all good and this is exuded outward thus giving purpose for our souls. These signs are the very essence of what we seek and we adhere our virtues to in order to grow sound in spirituality.

We all have the reflective values in us to absorb all traditional beliefs and we actually go a step further to acquire the self-realization to keep perfect harmony. The steps in which we travel our journey here in this life is always a building block in which we create the perfect us. The foundation upon what we desire the four cornerstones of, compassion, truth, understanding and love, are the key components in spirituality and in everyone's life thus begin your spiritual trek for deeper inner peace.

Signs from Heaven, is a composite of many inner thoughts and true feelings that are derived from true spirit and we all hold this very inner love, which should be expressed outward to continue the plight of true sharing in spirituality. We are all spiritual beings having an experience in a humanistic way and it is one of the most intriguing living absolute life's we have. Take heed to all around you; obtain as much information you can while absorbing the perpetual wheel of spirituality, making certain that when time comes that you have lived your life that has been full of inner signs to the exact extent that God has intended for you. Grasp every element of your true inner self and self-realization bringing it to the forefront for all to see, giving proper recognition that spirit moves in many ways not in one direction and become part of that spiritual train.

Preface

Signs from Heaven was inspired through the compilation of seminars held to teach those about the other side through our inner soul. Each intricate sequential part of this book deals with the reality of spiritualism from the ground up. Down to earth realism in spiritualism and its teachings of superb topics have been seen through many eyes at many seminars held throughout the years in the online chat room, in person, doing live shows on radio or television. Each topic deals with the utmost respect, giving virtue to the reader and offers that chance to actually reflect in most part about our inner self, our souls.

When glancing through the writings of this work one will find the intrigue to read and re-read many topics for it's a refresher course of the unknown brought to the forefront for all to enjoy. So much illustrates through the wordings of Robbie Thomas and leaves us all with wanting much more from the other side. Take hold of this book and let the intrigue guide you for the guidance one finds within the pages are that of *truth, compassion, understanding and faith.*

The bringing to the surface the ultimate in spiritualism and groundwork through spirit is felt among these pages that gear the reader for more and more. Search among your soul and find what is connected in the writings that will bring out every possible thought of and more than you can imagine. The four cornerstones of spiritualism are laid out for all to cherish, so without further ado, please enjoy *Signs from Heaven.*

Memory of Noelia

I had the pleasure to meet a kind-hearted lady who thrived on what the day brought her and her family. She wasn't about money or any prized possessions, rather of love from the heart. You could feel it from her, for it shined through her eyes and in her innocent smile. She was a quiet lady but strong with spirit; her face lit up the room as she entered and brought a sense of wellbeing to everyone she gazed upon. Noelia had two small children named Ligia and Vera, whom she loved more than life itself. Her husband Domingos was a very devoted husband and father, a man whom I had the opportunity to get to know on my short stay on the Island of Graciosa, Portugal. This was a very loving family, young and spirited, loved life and always gave back for every blessing they had been given them.

I was somehow drawn to them; I felt some sort of spiritual happening or something was to happen after my visit to the island but couldn't put my finger on it. My wife and I learned the news of Noelia's illness of liver disease through a phone call, which it was a progressive disease at that. Thoughts started to run through my mind as to, *what in the world could have happened to this lovely lady, who just loved life so much and her family? What could be done to assist them?* We started to get information about the hospital on the island as to the facilities were not able to care for her in any fashion whatsoever. The equipment was either outdated and/or they didn't have the medication to even alleviate the pain she was in. It left me feeling a sick empty vile spot in my heart that ached for more compassion from somewhere, someone to assist her and her family.

News of Noelia screaming in pain night and day from the dreadful disease that was now consuming her liver while other organs failing with no help in sight, no one to give proper medication or medical attention to her, left a terrible feeling setting in with me. From some insightful visit and inspiration from spiritual direction, feelings of helping were taking place and it seemed to be moving through me. Now if you ask me how I gathered all the names and contacts I am about to share with you, it in itself is a miracle that this all came about leading me and my wife down a road of hard, driven work for the love of a single human being.

I somehow managed a name or contact of a reverend that belonged to an organization that does work around the globe to alleviate poverty- or disease-ridden areas in many regions. This man who came to give guidance daily pointed the direction in which to take bringing us on a huge quest to conquer the misconceptions of human spirit, in which I mean this: that there are many great people out in the world doing great many things but a *sleeping giant* needed to be awakened and he stated that I was that little person who could do such a thing, he felt this.

My wife and I started our quest for knowledge, to find out who exactly would be willing to open their doors, pockets or their hearts for aid in this spiritual trek to find help for Noelia. Gathering our resources that we had, which weren't much at the time to assist in any way, we still seemed to be deemed fit to help out in any way. We managed to ring up phone bills as high as eleven hundred dollars and many hours spent on the phone waiting for calls back from high officials from around the world. The ball was rolling now; it seemed to be building speed with all the guidance of a single angel on earth, a simple man of the cloth, a loving caring reverend who each day put the fire right back under my seat to carry on another day to find the answers we so desperately needed to have for this loving family. Phone call after phone call, politician after politician, sovereign government after sovereign government, all of which were too much on accepting the fact that, *why should we help when their own country doesn't?* This struck me very odd as I started to gather more steam and anger inside, for now I was looking at the facts of different

12

scenarios. Those contacted actually used this family's country for gain in one sense or another in the past. A burr was sitting not well with me and that *sleeping giant* needed to be awakened and shown right in its face the true meaning of spirit, *human spirit.*

What struck me so odd was how fast and how egotistical some politicians are from many countries around the world and to think these are our great world leaders. Well let's start with the United States and the amount of senators I called up along with congressmen. While holding back their names I will also mention states they represented. The fact of Michigan has many representatives and I thought while our members of parliament have a good deal of dialogue also friendship, why not start there for also the Americans do have an Air Force base twenty minutes from Graciosa Island to Terceira Island owned by the Portuguese. This air base was very strategic in the first Gulf War, and I thought, *Well if they use the land of a country to kill thousands of innocent people as well as those who were not so innocent then they should or could offer to assist in saving but one good person at a tender age in her thirties.*

Well once I opened Pandora's Box so to speak, the giant was beginning to take notice of a small man trying to find answers. The type of answers I was looking for from those senators didn't surface; one senator, his office said, "If I paid taxes or did she, and then it would be a different story." They were "too busy trying to fix roads and help people of the State of Michigan, why would they go outside their country to help." Another senator of Michigan, his office said bluntly, "We don't care; it's not our place to save people," and these words echoed my mind and heart till this day. A congressman of Michigan was a bit more compassionate but still gave the run around as to wanting to help in any fashion whatsoever. It struck me very vividly in thought *if you can't offer them any residual help or pledge of any sort then you're not even a statistic but only a figment of their imagination.* I kept the phone calls rolling calling the White House looking for answers as to how can you use their land to actually run to the aid of the Israelis during the first Gulf War, which cost billions of dollars, yet only twenty minutes away was a lady if given the proper medical care could have been saved and that air force base had that primary care. I wanted answers from the great White House yet all I received once more was a big bureaucratic run around and told not to call there anymore. I guess there was no "oil" in her backyard for them to take as trade or maybe it was that the *spirit in mankind* those men who call the so-called shots, didn't have the time of day for a lovely lady who had two loving children who needed their mother and a husband who needed his wife by his side to see those children grow up and fulfill a lifetime of great memories. No, but I tell you this, those politicians all went home to their families, looking into the eyes of their children, holding their wives saying love you and building a future for a grand tomorrow. I understand that you just can't go out saving the world so to speak but this was a lesson and a calling from spirit that all this takes place as it was to unfold in front of my eyes.

What does it take to make the world see, if we don't start to care for a single human and yet shut the door to any conceivable thought of *resolve* for bringing peace to this world? Where is the spirit then? Where is the spirit within those dried up, old prune, withered away individuals who only have what's best for them or their lives around them in order and not what's at best for the entire world at hand? Where is it, I say? For it was stated long ago... "What does it profit a man if he gains the world but loses his soul?"...Jesus.

Day after day we would wait by the phone to hear any good news any great thought to come from the leaders of this great world. Calls were placed to the Israeli Consulate and I used the fact the American's had a vast interest in the Azores for it was Portuguese land those planes took off from to defend them from Iraq in the first Gulf War. They didn't take kindly that an individual was actually seeking help from them as well, just a helping hand to assist them to give her medical attention that would save her life and prolong it. I received phone calls back from the Israelis, which again it didn't give them anything back in order to help, but then again I wasn't done there; I insisted they look deeper for I would someday make it known that they only have one hand out and the other behind their backs the hand that should also be giving not hiding. They said they would be getting back to me once more, who in time they did and they asked me very vigorously not to speak of this that they wished me well in my endeavor to help this lady. Everywhere I turned it seemed if I didn't have some sort of hand out for the vast giant it didn't care who was dying and at any cost.

I even took it upon myself to call the Vatican, yes, that's right, the Vatican, and again was turned away with no direction even from the church of God. I do recall saying, "God never turns his back on us so how can you, Cardinal, say you will not help at all?" I played phone tag with the Vatican trying to reach someone more appeasing to talk with or someone who was touched by spirit whatsoever to step forward and listen to the status of Noelia. It's a very sad day when even the merciful church, the Vatican, shuts its doors on its own people and says "*no.*" *This be a lesson to everyone who reads this that God does love us all, Spirit does move through us, it's those who think they have the power to control every aspect of spirit or love of God we should be worried about.* I was dumbfounded to learn the last phone call back from the Vatican proved to be an ill feeling of disbelief and saddened to say a church that is to "reach out to everyone in any form to spread the word of God." God would have wanted help here; there is a reason I was given this trek to seek help and to see the results that were following each and every distasteful reply.

I actually got a great response from my own country, a country of very much love and understanding, which makes me proud to be a human being living in Canada. My local federal member of Parliament went that extra mile, cutting through red tape to have visas being drawn up for her and her hubby and a doctor from the Island of Graciosa to assist her to come and receive treatment in London, Ontario, Canada. Roger Gallaway and his office is a genuine fighting force for the humanistic spirit in all of us the spirit that comes from God. Rogers's office gave me hope to continue to go further and to move more forward to seek others that would reach out and say *yes, we care.* My heart went out now knowing, yes, there are spirited individuals who are willing to lend that helping hand and assist without compensation.

At this time now we are about three weeks into this quest to help Noelia and starting to find a light at the end of a very dismal tunnel. I started to find others were willing as well to assist us while I got a connection that helped me obtain free airline tickets from a Canadian courier to bring them over to Canada and a place for them to stay near the hospital. The spiritual feeling was growing and spirit was moving fast. We were so surprised to learn that a phone call I placed to a surgeon/doctor in London, Ontario, proved to be a Godsend! The doctor would perform any operation or treatment free of charge; he was a blessing that fell from the sky and things were just falling into place left and right now. Then another doctor called and offered to be the interpreter and assist in any form we needed him for as well. The heavens were actually opening up and the light was coming through; it was a miracle.

All that work and things were finally falling into place; God had sent his divine love to Noelia and to everyone who was about to embark on this remarkable journey. See it's not the size of a problem or the giant you face but the will of spirit and the drive you keep in your heart that makes all strong to carry on.

As everything started to flow properly in place and things were getting ready to be put into place we had an upsetting set back and our hearts fell further than you could imagine. Noelia ended up taking a turn for the worse passing away from the disease that so vastly took over her liver. It was such a terrible moment to swallow. How could this be? We were so close to having her receive proper care. My heart fell and I started to look back at all the events and the time I wasted trying to convince those mentioned above, the ignorant ways they portrayed themselves to me, for the lack of a better word, *immoral humankind.*

I tell you this story not to make you sad or to find hatred to those around the world who so selfishly refused to help but to see that no matter what, out of bad or where there is no spirit, God always finds

16

a way to shine through and show us, yes, never give up hope, keep moving forward. No mountain is too high or too big to move; the giant is but a little obstacle to overcome; spirit moves everything, and although Noelia passed on and left here two lovely daughters and a loving husband, the world was and is a better place for knowing her. I think if Noelia were here today she would say in her kind-hearted way *thank you to everyone regardless if they helped or not,* for it's not the amount of help one receives but just knowing people care enough to send love through spirit and this is what all is needed for good medicine in the world.

I often think of Noelia and her family. My wife and I speak of her often. For one individual to move another the way she did me and those involved showed me inside that no matter what in life you do or whatever befalls you, always love spirit for we are all spiritual beings from our loving Father who gives us the day in which we live. I treasure the moment in this life I had the opportunity to meet and share as much as a moment with Noelia for she has forever changed my views on humanity and spirit, which is a great thing!

God bless you, Noelia. May you rest in peace you deserve…Robbie.

Four Cornerstones of Spirituality

"Truth...Compassion...Understanding...Faith," four cornerstones of spirituality in which the foundation of everything in life is built. The solid ground upon which one builds their affirmations with spirit is the proving ground of strength and desire of knowledge. At no time are we lost or are we shallow without spirit; we only become displaced from time to time. We remain fully intact, for all the pillars to what we are stand strong within us; thus we are eventually put back on track gaining from every experience in life and what it has to offer. Reflection is a key to which we use to ensure the boundaries of all good to simplify any outcome and to adjust the setting within. Remember you are the fabric of life, the very essence to which spirit dwells; lift up your head each day and smile for all good smiles upon you!

The complete giving of oneself for another or for oneself. Spirituality shines through in the utmost respectful way when one devotes their heart of passion for lives here and life on the other side. Showing grace in all respect for each other is the accolade of unselfishness, which exudes proper heartfelt desire to grow in spirit.

Whimsical when finely touched upon that gives all resolve in any situation at hand. Capturing the ambiance and essence to knowledgeable conclusion, this will lead everyone to a most satisfied feeling of spirituality. Traveling the road of mapped out soul searching that grabs the heartstrings of all.

The refusal to accept anything other than what is your *right* and is *right* will leave your inner soul only seeking the purposeful light in which to grow in spirit that leaves no stone unturned. Only openness to accept without compromise to anything other than the absolute is the pillar upon which everything is built.

The proper way to show spirituality exists not only in writings but also from within oneself. The yearning to grow and learn, becoming a part in spirit for oneself. The true existence of the nurturing seed that brings forth the yield from within one's heart of hearts, your very own soul.

Chapter One

Departure Signs

If one looks at the way in which we live and marvel at the grace and beauty we are as spiritual beings having a humanistic venture, there are a whole lot of footnotes one could make. To include yourself and others around you in every course of life is to actually create those footnotes we so much reflect upon and take heed too. Search within and find where you like to begin each day, grant yourself the reprieve from all that burdens and look outward for the sign of spirit to show you your next bookmark!

It always struck me funny to say the least how we know our time has come. I mean it's not very difficult to surmise a situation of our loved ones who are about to take the journey to the other side. From the time of diagnosis or anything terminal we do have the understanding of the foreseen future at best. Those little signs that indicate departure time is close at hand, our loved ones do give us signals of them about to cross; it can be as simple as a burst of life coming back to them just before they leave. For example my grandmother on my father's side, she was ill and at a tender age. You could see that the life in her, she was tired and her will was going. Just before she passed a burst of life enveloped her, and she dressed up, looked forward to visits and even showed her emotions. This time period only lasted a short while and was a precursor to her time of departure. She took her journey home shortly after that; it left me with questions as I began a crash course on something new to me as a young child, warning signs. I thought about it over and over and tried to put into perspective as much as possible; I actually figured it out as I received all aspects of loved ones passing. This part of life intrigued me at an early age. I thought at times, *Wow, now if only we could see these signs, then why not stop the inevitable?* I began my own study you can say and realizing all that was of spirit to me, it was bigger than I imagined. After all I could see right, not quite, although ability has many aspects I was learning fast at an early age.

My other grandmother, well my grandfather and I had a talk and we discussed this issue on warning signs. He mentioned to me that the night before my grandmother had her operation she called him at home and said, "I think, big guy, you're going to be on your own now," and they talked a while and said goodbye as he explained to me. Well my grandmother passed that night and crossed over; she actually said her goodbye. Now on the other hand I became aware of her passing that night before the phone actually rang in the middle of the night. I awoke crying and I knew; then the phone rang and the news or her passing was sounded by screams of my mother. I explained this to my grandfather about my grandmother and I could see in his heart he acknowledged that I too was warned.

The spirit of each and every one of us is our source of power that keeps us going. Another example of warning signs I was favorably shown was my mother herself and what was about to become. The night before her passing I was visited and shown a vision and it was explained to me everything would be ok not to worry she would be fine. I went to my mother's the next day and explained to her exactly what I was shown. I had to, and I felt so compelled. I know she knew too but shrugged it off asking me to go home; she wanted to lie down. I will call you after she said. Well I received that phone call,

21

it was about an hour later she passed and she was on her journey back home. I believe in my heart it was her way of saying it's ok and letting go is a part of life and we all go through this.

Again continuing my talk with my grandfather he explained to me my mother actually stopped over to his home for a visit and told him goodbye. The way he explained it, he knew that she meant she was ready to take her journey. It was her last goodbye to him her father. As the tears welled up in his eyes I could see the whole last days of my mother once again. The most precious thing in life is life itself and to extend our love through sharing of our lives with each other from the moment of beginning to the actual departure like in the example of my family is the gift we give each other.

It is so strange, if I may say so myself, to as how the spirit actually connects each and every one of us and gives us our warnings. My grandfather actually jokes about how he listens to the obituaries on the radio to see if his name is being called. I laugh with him over this little injection of humor as we continue our discussion. A very wise man he is and I always look forward to a talk with him especially over a sensitive issue as departure times or warning signs if you will.

I do know when time comes for any of our loved ones to leave we are given signs; sometimes we just don't want to see them and tend to ignore any thought of it. It is our normal reaction to deny the inevitable, and who wants to lose someone close? No one does, so it is a defiance mechanism built in us that we tend to not see signs.

As my grandfather and I share our lunch together he reminds me that life is a blessing and we should always validate our love for our loved ones here before they leave; it's good for our souls.

I have given you some examples of warnings and how each is different from the next. You may have experienced similar or even different warning signs from your loved ones; it is a vast wall of love they do come to us and share that special moment of a new beginning. Our spirits or souls do control our destiny and the connection all of us is a magnificent aura of spirituality. We continually connect throughout our lives and from the other side; even during departure little signals are shown to us to validate the spiritual side of everything we have become. I am happy I had this discussion with my grandfather; it conveys the message of correctness to me about my so-called home schooling on departure warnings.

In one case I had a lady in the room and it was a normal day doing connections to the other side, when I was interrupted with a message of an older male that just passed and had crossed over. I thought this to be a strange; usually loved ones will introduce others or let others from the other side through to connect. I stopped the reading I was doing for brief moment to introduce the male so eager to say hi. After mentioning his name and his situation of his illness and other validations, the message was he had just crossed over and was doing fine. The individual this was for spoke up and in a confused and dismayed manner began to question everything I said. I assured her he was perfectly fine; he just wanted to say his goodbye to her and his love and admiration of her. She didn't take well to this and was visibly upset at the fact how could I say that. He did not pass; he was very much alive.

After being called everything from this and that she proceeded to leave the room really taken back at the fact I was saying such things and that I was wrong. Now everyone who was there that day witnessed this and were beside himself or herself as well. A few days later she came back to the chat room and apologized to me saying I was right her grandfather had passed; not only did he cross over but he passed and no one knew for two hours in her family after he did depart. She was the first to actually get the news via connection. She was very thankful for his coming through and the message of love he sent her and the warning signs of departure. The room was stunned and taken back to the fact the validation and message of him departing to the other side did actually come through the connection for her. I often speak of this reminding those who never had a chance to witness this reading that the spirit is so strong and always finds a way to show signs of departure.

Another time I was reading for a friend and the connection was with her sister who crossed over from a horse-riding accident. The connection focused around Jean's mother who was very much alive

23

and I was instructed to talk about Jean's mother and her upper stomach problems. As time went on it became apparent to me there was a message of warning signs with all the validation of Jean's sister's name and circumstances surrounding her passing. Jean even herself did mention it was a sign about her mother being ill. I do believe to this day Jean, bless her soul, kind of put those blinders on that refuse to hear any message or news of signs and it's perfectly normal as we all do. As the reading finished I had the insight of a warning sign of Jean's mother's departure or journey home and Jean's sister was actually conveying love and understanding that she would be there to greet her mother.

A week and a half went by and we learned of Jean's mother's passing and her journey home. The reading actually was a great reflection for Jean as it did bring her peace and understanding about the warning of her mom through her sister, Ann. It has given Jean strength knowing more and more about the other side and that her mother watches over her and her family.

The timing of warning signs are in a vast array of everything we come to know as life and the afterlife. It is a part of us as much as the sun rising tomorrow; we all get those heads-up warnings from time to time; it's how we choose to actually deal with them. In everything from life here and life there it's a small window or just a whisper I say away and we all are connected spiritually.

Another example of love and understanding sent in a connection that the warning sign of departure was close at hand is very evident in the next story. I had a connection to Jamie's hubby to be; he passed over and all validation of his name Danny and the way he passed were very evident. The rest of the connection surrounded Danny's mother, whom Jamie was still very fond of. The warning sign of departure was strong and the way it was is actually very interesting. During the connection Jamie was reminded to show Danny's mother the connection of love he was very persistent in her knowing he was fine. Jamie agreed to show Mary, Danny's mother, and she did. Jamie later explained to me Danny's mother had fallen ill and was that way for a while. I insisted to show her the connection and the

24

validations of everything we talked about. She came back a couple days later and also emailed me about Danny's mother. She said that she hadn't seen Danny's mother for a long time due to the fact of feeling guilt over his death; it just hurt her too much. She was compelled to show her the reading though and did so. She explained to me she read the connection to her while Danny's mother lay in bed in the hospital. I was also instructed by Danny to give Jamie the description of heaven I had written about so I obliged. Jamie read Mary this to her while she slept and when she finished Mary opened her eyes and said she was expecting her and that Danny had visited and explained that Jamie was coming. Jamie told me she closed her eyes after they talked awhile and drifted asleep. Jamie then left the hospital weeping not of sadness but of missing Mary and finding peace in her heart over the whole situation of Danny's death. She continued to explain that later the following morning she received a phone call; Mary had passed and was on her journey home. Jamie and Mary received love beyond any comprehension from Danny, not only bringing them back together but also easing the transition of departure for both.

The beauty of life is living it and to let live; it's the meaning of life. Everything that entails the essentials of life and its orders, all of which is allowed by God, is most certainly worth living. The phenomenon of warnings or departure times is as much a part of spiritualism and life itself and only gives credence to the life after. The signs of our loved one's journey that is about to begin is actually the precursor to a new beginning and in some fashion gives that let know situation that enables us to cope. Coping or taking heed to the information given us allows each individual to get their mindset ready for the inevitable.

If one sits and actually reflects back to a loved one in your family and the actual time frame they were about to cross over, the signs were there and in some fraction of a moment we can see we were told. Reflecting to look back at this is not a bad thing; you shouldn't feel funny about it. Actually the opposite feeling should be the quest for knowledge in the meaning of life and all about it. When we find life's little secrets, let's say, and we put into perspective everything we come to know and have been taught, isn't it sensible to say we all have the knowledge of the afterlife and about warning signs? It all comes from the teachings from God and everything is etched in our heart of hearts, our souls.

When I look into my children's eyes and I see the innocence and love, nothing but angelic virtues, I know myself when time is right things of this nature are not a terrible subject to discuss. Discussing warning signs of departure times, the signals of a beautiful journey is not shameful at all and no hesitation of doing so should ever enter your mind when time is appropriate. The world today is more now than ever awakening to spirituality and we all feel the presence of spirit. Everything we as humans come to know about life's beginnings and its so-called end here has much more information to offer us all and there is no shame in talking about any aspect of spiritualism and signs of departure.

There are many ways in which we get forewarnings and in our time of grief it is hard to comprehend everything coming at us from all angles. It's always good to talk and reflect everything about our loved ones before and after they depart, not to only acknowledge them but to learn, and if we say, yes, the signs were or are there, we are put at ease knowing we were warned. Through my study on this and having personal accounts of many departures it never stops to amaze me the amount of love the spirit has for us even when time comes for our loved ones to cross over. There is never the absence of love and understanding for each and every one of us when spirit engulfs all and cradles us. It's just one of life's many treasures if you will and we inherit all aspects of life's lessons, thus making everyone all students of spiritualism and eager to learn more about the afterlife.

All my life being able to foresee the inevitable from time to time and much more than that, I used to think *I was cursed*. In time and realizing of the good it could offer only re-enforced everything I did come to know; signs of departure is only a stepping stone to a sanctuary of infinite love and peace and allows all here to also

26

prepare for our loved one's journey. It's not a permanent farewell but a see-you-soon departure and we all will have some type of part to play so to speak when time comes for our loved ones or for us.

More than Signs

The spirit and will of many are a vast engulfed energy that brings good to everything spiritual. There are many circumstances that surround many happenings in one's life and most of which is spirit driven. When one looks at certain issues or events, which have transpired in their lives, you can see, not coincidental, but let's say earmarked timed signs. If you sit and ponder the point, reasoning for anything other than what is true spirituality and spirit, you're taking a logical sense of trying to determine anything but. There is reason for everything and if we go to the spirit of God, creator of all and everything, from day one it began with life and spirit from him.

Let's take a look at a circumstance of a sign and not a coincidental landmark happening. In my life alone there are many to which I am aware of spiritually and reminiscent of always. My mother and her brother, my uncle Doug, were very close and her passing took from him and we all could see. She passed at age fifty-seven in September 1994, a tender age that's for sure. Well she passed from cancer and we all know that is a dreadful disease. Now Uncle Doug was a good man and very lovable; well cancer also took hold of him, but what strikes me is he too passes over at age fifty-seven a few years after my mother did. With that said that is a sign in itself, but it gets better yet. My mother and my uncle not only crossed over at age fifty-seven each but both were the exact months away from their fifty-eighth birthdays. My mother passed in September and her birthday being in February; my uncle was born in March and passed in October. If you take the actual month they both passed and move forward to their fifty-eighth birthdays you will see each were 6 months equal to their birth. Now we have both passing from the same disease and at the same age and at the interval between passing and next birthdays. These signs come to us all and in many fashions it's up to us to look and reflect at how connected we all are in this life to the next to get

27

a clear picture of the times in which we depart to the actual signs of choice we leave for our loved ones.

Another sign of strong-willed spirit is driven to find happiness and one can say keep family happy. This unique situation I will share demonstrates the will of spirit and guidance given. My mother met my father and after six weeks of knowing each other they decided to marry, and the marriage took place five days before my mother's birthday. I never learned any particulars of this till after my mother's passing when we were all discussing her life. Well it struck me funny days later when I began to think about my own marriage and how my wife and I met. See the funny thing was I met my wife and after six weeks also we married and the twist is this: we married as well five days but after my mother's birthday. I hold this very dear and as a great sign because of the fact I did not clue in or was aware of this till after my mother's passing. Some may say both these fact-based stories I have told you are just coincidence and nothing more, but see the fact is, we are guided many times in our lives and from spirit, and when willed spirit intervenes and does good to show love and understanding, it's not coincidence, it's spiritual.

In the course of one's life and if you take a minute piece of it and examine spiritual signs and/or departures you will see the forewarnings were there and may have been overlooked or just not comprehended properly. Reflection of a loved one's life and everything that entails about them from beginning to end here in this life a picture of many spiritual events have occurred over and over. It's up to us here to do the examining of this part of life, draw our opinions and learn from it, for isn't that part of the meaning of life?

Other Signs from the Other Side

After all we have discussed and examined from departure and warning signs, well it doesn't end there. From time to time we are reminded from the other side with signs of love and guidance. Everyone can relate to this facet of life and can recall many encounters of signs. One afternoon I was talking to a lady named Patricia and there is a story that goes with her name as well. See

Patricia bought my great aunt's house from my sister named Patricia, which in turn my sister was given the authority to have the house from my great aunt and my mother named Patricia as well. What are the chances of that happening with all three named Patricia? Well as I continued to our conversation with Patricia, she mentioned to me my aunt was visiting her often. She started to tell me how she would vacuum the living room carpet and in a motion that the fibers would stand upright and create a soft look. Then she continued to say in the morning she would get up and see the footprints of my great aunt walking across her living room floor. She kind of took to my great aunt and has developed a liking to her giving her and our family signs of the afterlife.

Now I know my aunt isn't earthbound because she would also travel to my house and play with the brass lamp of hers I have by making it go off and on, flutter from time to time. She is only sending signs of the life from the other side. Again we can look at the names involved and what was meant to be, the signs of my lovely great aunt leaving her footprints to turning the light on and off. The presence of spirit and signs we receive from the afterlife are all part of this chapter departure signs.

Another sign of guidance from the other side happened when my wife and I bought our home we now live in. We were in the hunt for a new home to buy and it being our first we were very anxious and happy to raise our family. The market was tough and to find a home with four or five bedrooms in our price range was even tougher. After months of looking and no luck we gave up the search for the perfect home. A month went by and we just happened to travel to a part of the city we normally don't visit and especially the street. It's in a very nice area and back in from main roads; we never traveled that way when we took our children for car rides. Well didn't we come upon a house, a beautiful home, and we wanted it right that moment. We enquired about it and found that the lady who had it for sale wanted out and the price for that area was fantastic, and to top it off it was a five bedroom home. From the time of enquiring about the home and finishing the deal, it was just about two hours gone by. The realtor bent over backwards for us and even gave us a one percent cash back on the selling price to make it happen and we even bargained our way to two new appliances as well. Now I was amazed and I felt a very strong pull to this home and everyone who knows me when I have a strong feel for that there is more behind the scene here. I felt like there was something wrong and just couldn't place my finger on it, but nevertheless we had our new home. While signing papers with the realtor for the finalization of the deal we learned the reason why the home was for sale and why we got our price. Gina the lovely lady we bought the home from her mother and father had been in a fatal car accident just recently. Her mother and father were staying with her and remodeling Gina's home, because Gina herself had come down with cancer and needed help. My heart sank and I felt so deeply for Gina words couldn't come out right or I couldn't think of anything to say that would be proper. I just felt bad because of the circumstances.

After being in the home I began to hear whispers and footsteps at night from the bedroom of ours to the kitchen. I have stayed in touch with Gina off and on; during one of our telephone conversations I started to describe to her about visitors I knew we had and before I could finish my sentence Gina spoke up in a bit of a shocked manner and said what visitors. I knew it was really hard for her; I could feel the pain in her heart and also it still wasn't too long after the time her parents crossed over so I changed the subject to ease the tension. Those whispers led to things making noise at night, footsteps and even sitting on the edge of our bed. I feel her mother more so than her father but he too comes around at night; you can actually hear the converters for the televisions hitting each other from time to time.

The sign for Gina is in the writing of this for her; again our loved ones have purpose for all and in this little story I have been able to share with you just that. Signs come in many different ways and even while in chat I get told to say things that send the meaning of love to the receiver. One time I was instructed to say to a lady that she was at that very moment turning her ring on her finger; she was beside herself to learn that what she was doing at that moment was actually seen from the other side. The signs of life here and life there is only a thin vale, a whisper away. So the next time you are given departure or warning signs, take in the information and reflect about your loved ones for it's them sending those signs of love and understanding.

One thing throughout the years of actually reading for people, those signs of the departed often take us all back and really give the love and insight of the afterlife. From warning to departure signs there is so much more to look at and this does give a good perspective on the subject. To have such love from the other side and to have a glimpse of what is to come or to be guided to a certain place in life we all share the common goal in spirituality. The bond between the life here as we know it and the life on the other side never ends and always will show the way to our heart of hearts our souls.

Those little signs that we often receive from the other side gives each of us a chance to realize that life does go on and puts our mind at ease. A soft scent of our mother's perfume or a beautiful flower once adored, these are ways in which let's say a loved one will let us know they are around. The strong smell of a cigar or aftershave might be the order of the day in which we are again given the sign of a loved one around us. They never stop visiting or helping us in our everyday life; we are never alone and that also puts us at ease.

Let's face it, if you had the chance to show any sign at all to your loved ones here to ease the pain of them losing you or to let them know things are ok with you on the other side, wouldn't you seize the moment to do so? The same for them: they are always going to be family and never leave us to deal with life's hardships alone. Remember those little inner strengths we get are like little pick me ups throughout the day and keeps us going. Well those little pick me ups are spirit driven from our loved ones helping us along the way, guiding us with love and understanding.

From departure signs to warning signs we are all spiritually connected and have that link to everything in spirit. The sense of everything we are and have become is from the family unit of love and understanding, all of which again is from spirituality and from God. It's through this we learn to cope with love and life's ups and

31

downs; guidance comes from the other side in wavelengths astronomically huge, and it's only again a thin vale or a whisper away.

The next time we are down and we ask for a sign from our departed loved ones, that soft scent or that feeling of someone around us, they are actually sending us our sign not to worry, we are not alone, for love never ends; it grows.

Equip yourself with all the inner spirit you find deep within your heart of hearts, realizing the fact that we all come from the other side to this life as a journey of lessons in life. Consume everything throughout life as it will consume you in its beauty; the revelations of departure and signs of are all a part of everything we are. All the signs of life and the actual time to cross over from this life to the next are bookmarks in your heart and soul; it is but a refresher course for us all if you will. Reflect to the solitude in your heart, find that inspirational reverence, seek all answers from this life to the next, all the while keeping in mind that we are given the opportunity to witness the extraordinary results of signs.

Give way to the skepticism that may flow through your heart and thoughts for it only creates a premise of disillusioned attributes that neither is positive nor a creative step in spiritualism. In life's lessons and tribulations we all see forward, which entails proper thinking of the afterlife, thus leaving one with the utmost respect for spirit and oneself. Never disregard any sign or significance of what could be for everything you feel is inside your heart of hearts, the tools of precise measurement of spirit. Lend the credence where is necessary, for if one looks back on many times of loved ones passing over there are high profile significant signs that are given just before they take their journey.

When our loved ones begin to become aware of the significance of their journey at hand it's the will of spirit that takes over and the assurance is given to us the ones left in this life. It's the earmarked truth of life goes on, on the other side, and the presence of spirit is always around. If one reflects at a time of a loved one's departure you can feel within yourself the difference in the atmosphere around them and the gut feeling you have when time is present. We all carry that measuring tool of spirit inside us, for the spirit in us is of so much compassion the empathy and sympathy that drives us overcomes all other feelings and we become so much more aware of the situation. The feeling of lightness or the situation of it's finally relief we feel for our loved one surfaces in how we act toward them and to others. These are but hind-sighted circumstances that we will all go through and feel; thus if we actually reflect to a time before, during and then after they pass, we can see there is that spiritual connection that we all have and it is that awareness of departure that is painted before us as if a artist paints on canvas.

Chapter Two

Acceptance

Each day we thrive on what good intentions we can give and how are we going to be received in the venue of the day. Seeking approval or attention to make our way is only but a mere satire to each one's life, as we know it. What is the proper feeling and outward pouring of compassion can be felt through the forward movement and the literal thought of acceptance for all around you. Grant your inner self peace while alleviating all pressure that has distilled within through the acceptance of you and spirit; you are the only true ingredient that is needed!

Sometimes things in life become hard to focus or even unbearable to face, but in all of everyone's adversity we are a wonderful people. We have the underlying tendencies to override, overcome any challenge set in front of us.

The thing that grabs the heart of us all is the fact we have built-in mechanisms that say to each of us, we will overcome the inevitable and the outcome will resolve itself. All we have in life is desire, willingness and the settlement with ourselves to say, *yes, I accept the results of any position of any situation.*

When one accepts the warmth of love, understanding and

compassion, we become whole in spirituality and progress accordingly to what is the purpose of what is to be. To break off captivity of our souls, we relinquish all our inhibitions to what we should have over right of freedom and unadulterated pure understanding; we become in essence whole with life itself.

Thus having said this it leaves each and every one with the absence of squalor or wrongful ways and we breach spiritualism and embrace the light of God and spirit. Imagine rather than speaking of it, the fact you can embrace an individual without ego or a disposition of wrongful intention. Sounds hard; not really, it's all dealing with the acceptance of love, understanding and compassion, the fine ingredients and everything we have been accustomed to throughout our lives.

To be accepting means *to be enlightened; enlightenment is the acceptance of free will and an overture of the love of God and spirit.* The purpose of all is to have harmony and no discourse during one's life; this is set forth in the way we all come here from life on the other side or home if you will.

Spirituality has every comfort zone we all crave and desire throughout one's life without complacency. What do I mean by this? Well in spirituality one seeks the reverence of God and spirit and to find the happiness in one's heart. The fact of the matter is complacency is self-governed and in spirituality acceptance overrides the issue of anything less than that of union of spirit with all, not singleness. We do all require this throughout our lives in order to grow stronger in the sense of our very own initiative in spirit. Given the fact we all have compassion for human kind, the fact of acceptance, we should all become more aware of opening our hearts to each individual and let the light of spirit engulf our heart of hearts…our souls

Grasping the concept of life in its own light is hard for some to comprehend but it really is a cakewalk of sorts if we follow our souls' desires to have the acceptance we deserve and long for. Gaining spirituality is in everyone's mindset, and in accordance with free will, we become this regardless of any outcome fetching our capabilities of understanding, love, and compassion which is the transition of all good.

Believing and faith are steps that all take many times throughout our lives. Hence, we never lose our faith; we only take small steps throughout all of our lives, which is gainfully pleasant. If one can have acceptance on many issues of different perspectives, why then is spirituality an issue? It isn't; it is how one deals with their very own realism of the fact. In everything that has become and shown to all of mankind you would think *the knowledge would be overwhelming, pointing to the fact acceptance is the key to the very soul of us all.* We are from God and with spirit; we house all the rights to everything that is possibly known etched in our heart of hearts.

The concept of us having ability to determine outcomes or foresee the future events in our lives sound a bit far-fetched. Well it's not; we can do this by opening our hearts and the acceptance of life, love and spirit.

Look at your family; see how they are in your heart. Everyone knows we do foresee happenings due to the fact it's in us all to look ahead and plan. That is part of acceptance. Determining what God has set forth for us all and understanding this is called acceptance of many institutional giving's that we require and completely are accessible to. The determination of how to divulge this is to accept once again spirit in its entirety and love life itself.

Many times those that travel through the realm's chat room come with many questions pertaining to acceptance and look for a greater of realism that enables them to understand more. Drawing a line in the sand only limits an individual we need to expand our acceptance of everything from belief, faith, understanding and love for all. This is a widely discussed invitation to adhere our hearts to, the light of everything we seek, which enables those to participate to grow stronger in spirituality. Looking within the light, searching for answers lends credence to where, who, and why we have purpose here. Acceptance is in every part of our lives here and from there...home.

Grasping the thought of each and all are accepted by God

regardless leaves one humbled to the fact why are we a society that takes time to decide from day to day our right outcome.

Think of it this way: *to do what is right and our right is so much more meaningful to approve than it is to be non-acceptant of us.* Shredding that pride and egotistical ways and looking deep into your own gives total purpose of life. Accept it; it becomes you. Giving of oneself totally to life and what we have come to know as the ultimate experience in spirit we live life, as it should be. Reaching for the truth and seeking its message is for all; this is our purpose here in this life; take it embrace the light of God for it has been said, *"I am the way, the truth and life everlasting"*...amen

When one opens their heart and feels that void filled with such reverence and overwhelming fulfillment, it's a craving of desire, a belonging that dwells deep in the annals of one's soul. This permeates anything less than the emptiness one seeks on a quest to fill the knowledge of understanding. It becomes you once you feel the acceptance that runs through one's veins and leaves the etched markings of spirit within the walls of skepticism. The overture of love and understanding exudes through the very existence of you. Learning to cope or to even, say, struggle to understand is part of acceptance and we all share in this disability that renders us able to learn and adjust. Seeking the proper way in which one actually can convey their feelings as to what is taking place inside them is a journey in itself and will map out the course of your history in spiritualism.

Finding the ability to absorb such information or just to feel it is an undertaking and we all travel this road in our lifetime. Be not afraid for it is in each of us and all around us; we dwell in the house of God and Spirit and this is the assurance, which leads to the very aspect of acceptance. Cascade the thoughts of what we are; let them run through your mindset a bit and then take them and give them purpose of why are we spiritual beings. Let that everlasting light shine in your analogy of thinking and search your heart out for the bountiful but beautiful ending to the story you're telling yourself. Stop, grab hold of that feeling just now the one that directs your heart to say, *yes, I know now and it's true,* the feeling in me resides always etched in my heart of hearts…my soul!

It seems like a trek that is endless in the search or quest for the knowledge of understanding acceptance, but if we admirably give way to the notion of, yes, the purpose of me is to live and let live, and bring happiness around me, then why is it so that one disregards the fact spirituality exists in each of us. Fear, that's right, fear! The fear of acceptance is only the beginning, letting one become harmonious with spirit; something to one that isn't tangible and only sought after for a lifetime. Faith yields acceptance and acceptance becomes the faith in which every last soul desires and quests. It becomes set in stone as we all feel and love the understanding of spirit, becoming the flagship to many questions that are faith based and strong in the thinking of everything everlasting.

Acceptance is a part of our soul, a part of our life, a part of everything we have become. The outstretched hand of love, commitment, understanding and the truth lie within our grasp and is ours for the taking; it belongs to us our very own right. Examine freely and hold nothing back for if we don't question the fact of us and the way things are the truth may never be ours, for it's through that train of thought we all achieve the final result and we achieve acceptance always. Always look forward, I say, and continue to travel a straight path for that's where everything lay, in front of you, and in the conquering of our fears and doubts we all seem to lay the brickwork or the foundation instilled in us as a new formal greeting and introduction once more.

Remember as a child the fact you would look up to the heavens and have the wondrous thoughts cross your mind as to the picturesque place where angels sing and clouds of fluffy soft pillows lie. The absolute in any child's mind's eye and it burns that flame of hope and desire, the craving of wanting to know more. This is part of acceptance and we all crossed this path many times in our lives be it a child looking to the heavens or a gentle reminder to ourselves through a reading or sighting of spirituality in any form whatsoever.

In the up and coming reading the presence of spirit is so very overwhelming and gives direction and guidance to the receiver and the receiver's family. We often seek guidance in our hearts and we cry out in pain trying to locate the proper avenue to venture down and capture the reverence of good. Whether we are aware of it or not, the other side is always knowledgeable of situations here and occurrences that happen in our daily life. We never walk alone in the path of life, for we are led and guided given choices among our detailed scripted journey, which in turn we often seek advice without knowing but are so readily accepting of. Finding the strength to conquer the weakest elements that control us and/or the world around us is but a whisper away and backed by faith of spirit.

®»»·†·ŠØÜL·‡·MÄÑ·†·««®: hi hon

Sunshine: hello

®»»·†·ŠØÜL·‡·MÄÑ·†·««®: lol…who has the heaviness in the chest lower chest area

Sunshine: I do

®»»·†·ŠØÜL·‡·MÄÑ·†·««®: what's wrong dear

Sunshine: maybe my daughter too worrying about my daughter

®»»·†·ŠØÜL·‡·MÄÑ·†·««®: the stress causing you pain in your chest area and like cramping it hurts

Sunshine: yes

®»»·†·ŠØÜL·‡·MÄÑ·†·««®: this you have to stop worrying I know its easier said than done but I am feeling you and if I hurt I know what you're going through…it hurts

Sunshine: it doesn't feel nice

®»»·†·ŠØÜL·‡·MÄÑ·†·««®: no not at all, panic attack type it's going to hurt

Sunshine: plus I have a heart disease so it's not good

®»»·†·ŠØÜL·‡·MÄÑ·†·««®: you tried to get out and do a walk and breath deep fresh air a good 10 minute walk is good…who smokes around you

Sunshine: me

®»»·†·ŠØÜL·‡·MÄÑ·†·««®: male who smokes too

Sunshine: bad

®»»·†·ŠØÜL·‡·MÄÑ·†·««®: yes I smell it

Sunshine: my boyfriend too

®»»·†·ŠØÜL·‡·MÄÑ·†·««®: look hon that is no good either right now clean the air both of you should stop you heart not liking this and it's not good

Sunshine: I am putting it out

®»»·†·ŠØÜL·‡·MÄÑ·†·««®: I am feeling you and smelling things and it's no good you need a break go for a walk 10 minutes breath fresh air

Sunshine: my daughter is in a drug rehab… yes

®»»·†·ŠØÜL·‡·MÄÑ·†·««®: and it will make the pain go it will…your daughter going need a bit of love and understanding the crowd she hangs around no good at all

Sunshine: I really don't like being empathic…Feel it so much and always-sad things and stuff

Sunshine: yes I know they are no good

®»»·†·ŠØÜL·‡·MÄÑ·†·««®: the fact too I have there are two guys that bother with her too much and this is her downfall

Sunshine: do you get any names?

®»»·†·ŠØÜL·‡·MÄÑ·†·««®: these two guys are the reason to hang and be cool

Sunshine: they are all bad

®»»·†·ŠØÜL·‡·MÄÑ·†·««®: yes they are all bad…Chris's name comes up for the good side

Sunshine: drugs

®»»·†·ŠØÜL·‡·MÄÑ·†·««®: you know this name Kris or Chris

Sunshine: her brother is Chris

®»»·†·ŠØÜL·‡·MÄÑ·†·««®: ok this male is also acknowledgeable of this so he knows what's going on and something does she talk to him about things

Sunshine: doesn't talk to him a lot I don't think he doesn't live where we do

®»»·†·ŠØÜL·‡·MAÑ·†·««®: ok this Chris is very aware of her though something about this here his name comes up

Sunshine: ok I know he hates drugs

®»»·†·ŠØÜL·‡·MAÑ·†·««®: I was going to say maybe that relationship should be redeveloped like bring them together more he can be good influence on her

Sunshine: that's good

®»»·†·ŠØÜL·‡·MAÑ·†·««®: can that be arranged

Sunshine: she's 17 he's 27

®»»·†·ŠØÜL·‡·MAÑ·†·««®: I get angels so this means like it's a good idea its good

Sunshine: ok

®»»·†·ŠØÜL·‡·MAÑ·†·««®: he can be her mentor he can help her the more he gets involved too in the life of you guys the better and show her a lot

Sunshine: my bf tries to help her too

®»»·†·ŠØÜL·‡·MAÑ·†·««®: good but I bet if Chris was there more it would be good

Sunshine: ok

®»»·†·ŠØÜL·‡·MAÑ·†·««®: have a talk to him see if he will help

Sunshine: yes I will

®»»·†·ŠØÜL·‡·MAÑ·†·««®: and not in a way of doctor but like a friend

Sunshine: ok

®»»·†·ŠØÜL·‡·MAÑ·†·««®: she needs this

Sunshine: yes I know she feels alone

®»»·†·ŠØÜL·‡·MAÑ·†·««®: Yes

Sunshine: she thinks I am the only one who cares about her

®»»·†·ŠØÜL·‡·MAÑ·†·««®: and with him he can

help she will respond you will see guarantee

®»»·†·ŠØÜL·‡·MÄÑ·†·««®: GOD BLESS YOU

Sunshine: thank you

®»»·†·ŠØÜL·‡·MÄÑ·†·««®: YW HON

From: Tammy

Sent: October 28, 2004 8:06:25 AM To:
Robbie Thomas

Subject: A READING ROBBIE DID FOR ME
ABOUT MY DAUGHTER

Hello Robbie,

I would like to thank you for a reading you did for me on October 15th 2004. Robbie had picked up on my daughter Danielle she is 17 years old. When Danielle was 12 her father passed away from cancer he was only sick for a week and passed away. When she was 14 she was babysitting for a friend and the husband came home and raped her. He is in prison right now. Last winter 2003 she had a miscarriage. She started taking drugs and was hanging with the worst of people.

Robbie had picked up that Danielle was hanging with two guys that were influencing her into taking drugs. The worst of drugs she was taking. He also said that Dani should get involved again with her older brother who is 27 and that he could help her. When I went to visit Dani at the drug rehab place. I asked her Dani who are the two guys that are influencing you with these drugs you were taking. She just looked at me and said how do you know? So I asked her again. And she said how do you know and Mom you are freaking me out. She told me who they were. She kept asking me how do you know? I just told her I have connections. Robbie's reading told me this.

Robbie also picked up on the heaviness I felt in my

chest. I was feeling so stressed worrying about her. He also picked up on smelling smoke and I do smoke cigarettes. Which is not good for me at all. Also, that I should get out and walk. And that it will make me feel better. Which I do know I should be doing. I have just been too lazy to do it or not feel like it. Robbie also picked up on the name Chris. Chris is my son. Robbie told me that Dani should get involved again with her brother, which I did tell her to do, and that he would be good for her and will help her with getting off the drugs and will help her in her everyday life I believe. I would like to say thank you to Robbie for his help. I appreciate it very much. It gives me faith that one day soon my daughter Danielle will get better and will be able to overcome her drug addiction and that she will be happy again in her life. Some things you just can't talk about with people they just don't understand. Talking about readings and connections.

They think you have lost it LOL. But in Robbie group in chat you can talk about the things that are bothering you and troubling you and they listen. They understand. They don't think you have lost it LOL. I would like to ask you if you can spare some time to pray that my daughter Danielle gets better very soon and all her troubles will go away and she can overcome the things that are troubling her. I love my daughter very much. I love all my kids very much. I had to make her move out of home about a year ago. Because she was hitting me and I just didn't know how to deal with it. She lives in a foster home right now. I feel guilty about making her move out. But I just didn't know what else to do or how to help her. I am empathic and I feel what people feel. I find this very hard. I have to find a way to release the feelings I get for people. I feel them like they are my own feelings. When they are not my feelings. I know that with my daughter I feel them more because she is my daughter.

Thank you to Robbie for your help and everyone else in Robbie's group for just being there when you need someone to talk to.

Have a wonderful day and thank you again.

Sunshine (Tammy)

Acceptance comes in many varieties of ways and from spirit we tend to take heed a bit more from the influential aspects of being shown our lives in front of us from another. I do believe Danielle had a taste of surprise with the flavor of the other side seeing into her life. My guides have never failed me nor has the spirit of God; together it is one heck of a loving team to have on an uphill battle that is always won with unconditional love. The properties of everything we come to know about us, if we glanced once in a while inside us and realized that there is more to each of us and therefore respect all and everything even the temple of which God lives in us, we will become more detailed in spirituality and appreciate the finer things in life. For Tammy, I believe she will have her daughter back and a great child she will be; the growth of one's heart is measured in the love we have for each other and ourselves.

Acceptance of the other side has flourished in this reading and given a different perspective to help me. I am desperate for answers and guidance. It seems to be the little ingredient that we need every so often that makes the entire potluck of spiritualism seem so much more worth seeking. Faith is the driving force in which we all endlessly quest for knowledge and absolute in this life and we share this will everyone to gainfully express the true meaning of us all. In the end as you saw with Danielle's reaction to her mom about receiving the information to which she was speaking of, those individuals who were the bad influence I truly feel will no longer be a part of her life anymore. As for Tammy, the actual part of acceptance in the form of love for her daughter and in spirit has been overwhelmingly inspired and is transcended in her connection with the power of the other side.

Giving perspective to each of us is in the very depths of us; I know I harp at looking within you to find the essence of the truth behind spirit because it is part of us all. This is a great pillar of thought and a standard set long ago before we all came here to this life, for which we should always revisit to discover the groundwork laid by every soul that has crossed and enlightened us all. Respect is the grandest gesture to God and Spirit and it reflects the ominous wellbeing of everyone and everything; life is resurrected many times throughout a course of a lifetime and it has the making of a new beginning each day.

Every day we seek to find the proper way to see further and want a sign for heaven to say yes, we are in the right mode of things. Some feel that acceptance is necessary to move forward and that is perfectly right and others seem to have a hard time in the realization part of it for they seek too hard wanting the results in an anticipated way.

®»»·†·ŠØÜL·‡·MÄÑ·†·««®: angel hon who had chest problems here hon and the way I get it is I feel my lungs like very hard to breath and for some reason too hon my index finger hurts bad to me is there someone missing a finger hon

¥Ángèl òf Dèlíght¥: me Soul yes Soul My Mom had FINGER MISSING

®»»·†·ŠØÜL·‡·MÄÑ·†·««®: sorry had to get your attention this person hon I have… you have it yes omg

®»»·†·ŠØÜL·‡·MÄÑ·†·««®: and that's how I get the thing about this someone is showing me this right now

¥Ángèl òf Dèlíght¥: I feel it

®»»·†·ŠØÜL·‡·MÄÑ·†·««®: the thing I have too hon is my back of my head area hurts I have pain in my head

¥Ángèl òf Dèlíght¥: yes she died of blood clot in head

®»»·†·ŠØÜL·‡·MÄÑ·†·««®: right so hon this is coming to an anniversary of sorts here very soon some type of celebration some type of anniversary that involves her to you

¥Ángèl òf Dèlíght¥: my birthday

®»»·†·ŠØÜL·‡·MÄÑ·†·««®: and it is the fact hon of this person or for this person

Kurly: soul is doing a reading…sit back and listen and enjoy

Amethyst: right on I love when he does this

Tetley: souls reading…

¥Ángèl òf Dèlíght¥: my birthday on the 18th in a few days!

®»»·†·ŠØÜL·‡·MÄÑ·†·««®: great so that is her to you your birth and this being the 12th of the month

¥Ángèl òf Dèlíght¥: yes

®»»·†·ŠØÜL·‡·MÄÑ·†·««®: the way she came to me was with all the features hon of what is wrong with her at time of here… your validation

¥Ángèl òf Dèlíght¥: and they are true so very true

®»»·†·ŠØÜL·‡·MÄÑ·†·««®: been waiting long time for this you have

¥Ángèl òf Dèlíght¥: yes that's why I didn't answer couldn't believe it

®»»·†·ŠØÜL·‡·MÄÑ·†·««®: and why do I get some type of I would call it hold out to the last minute type thing did you guys play on each other like this before it's a funny thing not a bad thing but in order to clarify this

¥Ángèl òf Dèlíght¥: yes we were always laughing

®»»·†·ŠØÜL·‡·MÄÑ·†·««®: I have to know you two have something in common too something you share not because your daughter and mom but you actually share something

¥Ángèl òf Dèlíght¥: ? Like what?

®»»·†·ŠØÜL·‡·MAÑ·†·««®: I am being told like you have birthmark hon, something of a birthmark ok this is from that too but where does share something in common come from its like I went from birthmark and to shared something so either she had one too and this is what she is getting at

¥Ángèl òf Dèlíght¥: yes…yes on my shoulder

®»»·†·ŠØÜL·‡·MÄÑ·†·««®: what is March hon month of March

¥Ángèl òf Dèlíght¥: her wedding day

®»»·†·ŠØÜL·‡·MÄÑ·†·««®: your dad is there too right on the other side I have this he is with her

¥Ángèl òf Dèlíght¥: yes… yes… yes

®»»·†·ŠØÜL·‡·MÄÑ·†·««®: acknowledgement of this hon of them all what we have for you today is what you want to see and hear

¥Ángèl òf Dèlíght¥: my tears are flowing

®»»·†·ŠØÜL·‡·MÄÑ·†·««®: this is for you and there is much love here for you

Tetley: (((((((((((((((angel)))))))))))))))))

¥Ángèl òf Dèlíght¥: thank you

®»»·†·ŠØÜL·‡·MÄÑ·†·««®: you have never given up hope or anything this is for you

¥Ángèl òf Dèlíght¥: never

®»»·†·ŠØÜL·‡·MÄÑ·†·««®: very patient

¥Ángèl òf Dèlíght¥: thank you dear Soul

®»»·†·ŠØÜL·‡·MÄÑ·†·««®: well hon she is around you and you asked something of her when I get this its like a question mark so you must have asked her something

¥Ángèl òf Dèlíght¥: to save a place for me by her side

®»»·†·ŠØÜL·‡·MÄÑ·†·««®: angel hon you have long life yet hon I am going to make sure of it not your time yet hon that's what I get from her

47

¥Ángèl òf Dèlíght¥: tytytyty

®»»·†·ŠØÜL·‡·MAÑ·†·««®: what you're going through she is there she is and he is at your side... he is very quiet your father...quiet man I see, she is doing all the talking here.

¥Ángèl òf Dèlíght¥: then I will survive...yes he was very true

®»»·†·ŠØÜL·‡·MAÑ·†·««®: you're in great company hon very good hands big hearts to you I see big hearts for you lots of love

¥Ángèl òf Dèlíght¥: wonderful

Amethyst: my tears of joy for you angel

®»»·†·ŠØÜL·‡·MAÑ·†·««®: your keyboard make a funny sound when you type like a rattle, if you type fast does it make a funny sound

¥Ángèl òf Dèlíght¥: my tears are falling...yes it does yes

®»»·†·ŠØÜL·‡·MAÑ·†·««®: this is being shown to me hon so for me to have it it's from her to you she is with you

®»»·†·ŠØÜL·‡·MAÑ·†·««®: GOD BLESS YOU HON

¥Ángèl òf Dèlíght¥: God Bless you Soul...God Bless

Tetley: huge hug for angel

Kurly: huggggggs angel...that was so nice for you

Amethyst: (((((angel))))

¥Ángèl òf Dèlíght¥: yes it was and worth the wait

®»»·†·ŠØÜL·‡·MAÑ·†·««®: (((((group)))) Mac: (((((((soulie)))))))

Mac: (((((((((group)))))))))))

Tetley: wow that was awesome

ROBBIE THOMAS

From: Louise Heathcote
Sent: May 13, 2004 6:02:52 AM
To: Rob Thomas
Subject: Thank you Robbie... Angel of Delight

How can I put into words the wonderful thing that happened to me in the Community yesterday, I had waited many month's then suddenly there was my Beautiful Mammy and my quite Dad coming to me through Robbie, it was the most wonderful experience I have had I could not believe when Robbie said Angel who has a finger missing and now a pain in my head, Mammy died with a blood clot on her brain and she had a finger missing, then he said now I cant breathe that was my lovely quite Dad (smiles) ,I cried many tears but was happy too as Robbie could feel all the love for me and I felt they were holding me I was so warm ,it was beautiful ,....and Robbie I couldn't think yesterday I was so happy to be near them again the something in common you talked about Mammy did have a Birthmark too ,.......how do you thank a wonderful caring sensitive man like Robbie ,....he thinks only of how to help other's and he certainly helped me ,.........God Bless you Robbie ,...................Louise

Sometimes spirit moves in mysterious ways; we are so lucky to be given a chance to be able to connect and have such a lovely moment spent saying hello. When our hearts are filled with the positive of energy and the ever-lasting love of the other side we gain from everything that is our right to see, hear and feel. To have been able to successfully share in a loving moment from the other side with Sheila, bringing her parents through is a great day indeed. With the part of acceptance here is the knowing of patience and the will to withstand the test of time to seek out the truth of the other side and

49

bring forth resolve in one's heart knowing we are loved unconditionally. Louise waited a lifetime in respect to hearing from them and it all began with acceptance in her heart; this was the mountain that she climbed and when she reached the top she made the mold that shaped her presence in the heart of spirit. Acceptance is the enlightening spiritual right to all; we belong to spirit and are from spirit.

Louise's real first name is Sheila; she later went on to take ill and pass away as I found out, and this broke my heart for she was such a beautiful living human being in this life. She would always come into the chat site so happy to see us there kidding and joking full of life; a special person she was and still is for now she is the angel she so lived up to be with her nickname she gave herself. I learned of her passing from her husband who contacted me through email, which took a lot for him in this time of need. To him I owe a lot for he took the time to come and let us know we lost a dear friend who was stricken with a terrible disease.

John is a very admirable man. I thank you, John, for sharing with me your thoughts and words of your wife. You are a truly blessed man for having shared such a beautiful life with your Sheila, and we are blessed as well for the time we spent knowing her in this life. She truly lives up and has to the persona of being that "angel" whom we also came to know. She was a big part of the Realm chat room and will always remain that way…forever. John and I became quite acquainted with each other through mailing each other talking about Sheila and I had a surprise for him. I only ever read Sheila once, and that is the reading you have just read. John was a skeptic, if you will, to the thought of psychic ability and such but after I presented him with the reading of his wife it felt this was a message left for him and when the time was right it presented itself. I emailed John this reading to which he read and commented on feeling a bit taken back to a good stance with what had transpired. He writes me in a letter that I will now share with you.

Dear Robbie,

Thank you for your thoughtful e-mail it is always nice to hear from you. I am writing to you in regard to a reading you did for my late wife Sheila Louise. You truly thrilled her with your remarkable accuracy; you're right on so many things. I would like at this point to bring to mention you said that Sheila's mom had a finger missing on her hand, no one outside of her family could have known this. I find this extraordinary, truly I do, no one in a million guesses could have got this fact right. I am a skeptic but 'you truly gave me food for thought' one thing I must say Robbie.

My Sheila was seriously ill, in my heart I know that you, you personally gave her a great strength and I know that in Sheila's heart, she left this world and knew she was going to meet her beloved Mom and Dad and her son Chris.

In a personal note to me, John thanks me and I return the thanks to him…God Bless you John.

In the chat site I had an individual join up and it was but a couple days go by in which I started to have a draw to her and felt someone coming through for her. She asked me to kindly take a peek at a picture of hers she posted of her son, her and some others from a child's soccer team I was inclined to do so. After I glanced at the picture I started to receive messages of an older lady her mother who had passed and from chest problems. I returned to the room and started to question her and give her facts of and about her mother that she would only have known. She became a bit quiet and was responding but in a shocked manner, for here is a guy she just read about in the newspaper that has a gift and uses this gift for communication with the deceased. I don't blame her sometimes I come off real strong, which in turn I blurt out all information I receive as soon as I receive it. I started to see what was developing for her, countless informational images and dates, which in turn I relayed to her.

She seemed a bit off on this but in a way that she was gob smacked at what was thrown at her. I felt she needed the assurance of the other side after all she was on a quest to see if someone would help her communicate with her mom. Rhonda was able to be put in touch with her mother and the assurance ran deep for all that she was given was validated through the love of her mom from the other side. Rhonda has since then become a regular in our chat site and growing in spiritualism that has enabled her to not only see her growth but growth of others as well. Rhonda writes a validation letter to me, which I am including here for you to read which expresses the unconditional understanding of acceptance that she so desperately sought.

From: Rhonda O
Sent: September 29, 2004 8:07:22 AM To:
Robbie Thomas

It all started with a page out of the newspaper. I read the article about this man that "got rid of spooks" and decided to check out his website…. Ya da, ya da, ya, I joined and entered the chat room and talked to some wonderful, insightful people. The next day's conversation led me to post a picture of my son's soccer team with a questionable spot in the picture. Which Rob confirmed what was in the picture was a truly an orb. Cool… I thought.

Enter back in chat room. Chit chatting away and he asked, "Who is the older female energy was that passed away from heart failure?" Gasp, I told him "that's my mom!" He validated that she had this condition that we were all aware of and that's how she passed and not to have any guilt with her passing.

Rob then validated two birthdays in one month. That is my birthday and my son's birthday both in July one with a sore left arm...around the bicep area. That I still don't quite get. However, if I were to go out on a limb, if I may and say that I did put a temporary tattoo on my son, on his left arm, on his bicep...Which he just removed the other day. Am I pulling at strings here? Who knows?

I was told to look in other photos to see if I could find these so called orbs, which I may have overlooked. Before my reading I only ever found one suspicious spot in a picture, which I forwarded to Rob. I was then asked to look through prior photos only to find many other pictures with this same strange and wonderful spots. The pictures previously taken always included family members or my children.

The only thing that I needed to know from Rob was that my mother was okay. I already knew the answer, but what a wonderful feeling to have someone validate it for you.

Kudos' to you Rob!

Thanks Again
MidniteDixie ...Rhonda

Spirit has a grand way of letting us know and giving that subtle assurance when we need it most. For Rhonda, she received her assurance, thus leaving her with an understanding of the other side. It's a great feeling to help others out when called upon; it not only gives a perspective of the other side but a true meaning of spirit. Unconditional love has no boundaries; loved ones cross those boundaries from the other side many times in our lifetime to bring us that assurance we so desperately seek. Never stop asking questions or searching for the right answers; everything and all the tools lay within your heart of hearts, your soul. Our hearts yearn for this, the burning desire to the quest of knowledge; therefore keep every avenue open in spiritualism for spirit will answer your plea.

"From the moment of life's conception, there has and always will be the spirit of God the Father Almighty Creator of Heaven and Earth. As pure an innocence of a young child's love, we stare into the heart of spirituality and embrace the arms of spirit. We are engulfed in the Holy Light that becomes us forever more from this life to the next"...Robbie Thomas

Chapter Three

Healing of Our Soul

Imagine the thought of wanting to feel rejuvenated, the pleasure it brings you and others. Finding the joy of all for all starts within; this is the avenue to every success story we hear about. When we feel spiritual or the need to reach for spirit, a great force of absolute becomes us. Therefore we are the driving force in our own lives. Touch upon the very essence of you, seek the truth in every matter and when you find that comfort zone invite it in your very depths of your heart warming the inner soul. Become full in blossom and the scent of spirit will ring through giving you ambiance to which heals all!

Imagine you're having a great day and all is going so well; everything that emanates from you has such an aura of greatness. You feel so wonderful nothing will ever bring you down and anything you do or seem to touch turns to that so-called *golden glow.* Your heart is so lifted and at peace, the world spins and you're enjoying the great ride of the century. Everything can fall apart all around you yet it still wouldn't have an effect on your inner circle of understanding that you're such on a high and life brought you there. A storybook of events and still you're looking for the end that seemingly is not in sight for you are on a pinnacle of pure angelic goodness that exudes every yearning breath. You want to reach out, shake the world, give it a new cause to be alive and share in the deepest of revelations that can be felt by man, happiness for all for it is a burning fire within you to feel this way.

What you have just read is a powerful feeling, which we have all crossed this many times in our life and we will still revisit it again. It's funny how we always have the tendency to have highs and lows in our life, but at each intercept or conception of pain and disbelief, we always bounce back having this fortitude in us to move forward.

Grab for that brass ring and hang on to it; there is more to life than just being miserable or feeling down to a point where everything that crosses your path you are blind to. We all have that inner strength to carry on moving mountains while it's finding that absolute and creating our own safe haven, if you will, in order to eliminate all negativity from ourselves. There is nothing wrong whatsoever in this life of yours to search for the correct solution that will steer you proper in the plight of happiness. Creating your own sacred world seeking out institutional loving warmth for your inner soul while caressing the thought of moving forward should and will cross the broad scheme of things eventually. There is no right or wrong way to start healing but there is one thing that should be kept in the forefront and that is *you!*

You are the number one thing in life that matters to you; now with that said it is shown in you when you want to just scream it out why me...while you shake your fist at the heavens. Right there you are exasperating the thought process of self-reliance and the searching technique has begun to filter into your quest for peace. It's not wrong to ask for these types of validity in your life or is it wrong to have such anger built up after all it's all part of the *healing progression* that we all endure. You may think all those cliché thoughts of *why me*, it always happens to me, or anything at best my life really does suck! This should be looked at as a great thing though. See the fact remains this is the start of a fantastic voyage of inner soul searching that will eventually lead you to a viable solution and a great healing will occur.

When we all think of our life and do the reflection scenarios, we always seek the avenue that best suits us to heal fast and grabbing that sign that says, "enter here and have a great day." Our heart of hearts desire completion and the expulsion of anything utterly wrong in order to give us the proper enlightenment, which is our right to obtain through spirituality.

Healing is a natural element that is a driven gearbox, if you will, that gives us directional virtues to grow in peace and harmony with everything we come to know in our lives. The ultimate satisfaction that we can make a difference and the difference is us, for our lives do count and we are number one and given the love of spirit from God. In the midst of the darkest day...God's light will shine and help us through our hour of need...open your eyes and reach out your hand...he is there! Amazing and it's true for we all have the right to our beliefs, which is given from God. This enables us to move forward to conquer our fears and upsets and put an end to disbelief and relentless misery.

An analogy would be this. The branches on a tree that stretch out is it not for are they in charge of their lives and the growing process, so are we in the ever clear of life, which we hold the key to a successful growth in us.

Amidst the redundant feelings we possess of hate and anger will it not only lead us to the virtue of dismay within ourselves? Why not seek the love of say a garden, see the life in which it contains all beauty of the almighty? A true sense of life and the absolute in the structure of healing is to venture in another direction to absorb the substance it brings to you giving healing a great chance.

Key to success in healing is to actually have a vivid summation of your intentions and demands set on yourself that are proper while being logistical to carry out a plan that gives you room to love you. To actually say I will keep a mindful record of my actions is a case in point that this is true but wouldn't it be on a grander scale of things to actually write out your plan setting goals for yourself to enable that inner person of you to actually feel again.

Resourceful thinking and actual mindful thoughts for you to act on gives way to any premonition of maybe so or *I could have done that.* Seek what is proper in your heart and never give up hope for everything in life is built on hope and the human spirit. Making a record of your trials and tribulations in a journal of peace offerings to your soul gives way to any hardened resentment that may find its way in between the pages of your heart. Create that premise for healing; show yourself as you write it out that you're making those right moves to enable the distance between all that despair fall away. Now you're seeing the horizon of faith and hope. When you etch the memories of anything onto permanent markings you're actually releasing those tendencies of anything binding you to a horrible experience building a definitive way in which our hearts want us to grow. Taking those scripted events or detailed information that you have just earmarked for a release, make it the example of such.

Whenever you wish to rid yourself of the indulgent unnecessary controlling reminders just scribble them down taking the moment to eventfully do the actions of tearing them up saying to yourself, *I rid my heart of this ache and now start a new balance within.* The permanent actions you have just taken forth gives the visual of intent to you allowing your inner soul to react properly in accordance with spirit to heal.

We all crave the healing process that allows us to flourish and blossom in the light of spirit; thus this gives the strength of soul to shake the undesirable essence we have obtained. Nothing more so than to have a doctrine of your very own that shares your inner beliefs and loving ways, then to write out the problematic things we so much want to shred from our very lives. Give yourself the fighting chance to find the resolve, a resolution so sought after in your life bringing it to the forefront of your thoughts while escaping them by creating that script of dismissal.

The creation of life is a vast array of beauty in that beholds the eye of God who holds you dear to him; this is the foundation from which we all have our driving force. Never ever think that reaching out is a wrong solution in any event whatsoever, for it is the strength of many that gives way to the weak thus making them much stronger for who they will become. Individuals who are like-minded offer the reprieve of your ill-winded feelings to help heal you; this is a great start as well. Reach out giving those close to you a chance to set forth a works of invited loving feelings for you, taking advantage of everything given to enable you to gently move forward in healing. A person who lends that open hand of acceptance giving way to the openness of their hearts is a comfort zone to say the least. Embracing those who embrace is a sign of undoubted healing for the heart craves the attention it seeks from others as well.

Prayer is an excellent way to say let me be free from my burden, lift me up Heavenly Father grant me the peace I seek. God never leaves our side and always is the light in the distance for us to follow the right path. Why not talk to him, and give him the day's events that make it hard to carry? God gives us the day to live and let live; the rest is what he wants us to do, calling upon him to lighten the load, thus creating our own serenity of peace in us.

Reaching for scriptures, reading them to enlighten our days, making our nights less heavy, is a great way to exude the peace we seek. The word of God is the most tangible realistic love we can find for it is written, "We are his children." Imagine that now, we have a structured belonging so now we can actually set our minds at ease, for the fact remains we belong to the most heavenly spirit ever: we are a part of God. Healing has many aspects to endure but we never walk alone in this life, for we are guided and protected.

The Serenity Prayer

God grant me Serenity to accept the things I cannot change,
Courage to change the things I can, and
Wisdom to know the difference. Living one day at a time;
enjoying one moment at a time;
accepting hardship
as the pathway to peace.
Taking, as He did, this sinful world
as it is, not as I would have it;

trusting that He will make all things right
if I surrender to His will;
that I may be reasonably happy in this life
and supremely happy with Him forever in the next.
...Amen

The power of prayer, scripture, poetry or anything that gives your heart peace and the desire to move forward is a great source of strength to draw from. Giving of oneself to a higher expression of love and spirit is a great way to start a healing process for anyone in any situation.

Books are a great place to search out help as well grab a resourceful intriguing piece of literature that gives guidance or lends that ear to help you create the right mood for healing is a great venture. Our soul's desire to be complete, having the ambition to create wholeness for us to be as one in union with spirit is a most certain foundation building thought. Open your heart reach out accept what you can do for yourself seeing inside you are number one that you do count, for God made you count. Those doors that seem so closed making you feel shut off to the world, well bust them open and crossover the threshold making you the most important individual in your life. Healing begins with you; it is a part of you. Realization may take time but once you accomplish this take the steps to free you from the burden of ill will. Resolve is in sight and at your grasp. Reach out; grab it. It's yours for the taking, for you are worth it.

Seeking a reprieve from anything that will heal your soul or give you virtue to grow is understanding and the meaning of love. Soothing or mending fences, let's say, will create a premise for a certain growth in your spiritual realm. The heart will grow fonder, fonder for the finer things in life that drive the very essence of your core to experience the true meaning of you. Every aspect of healing growth begins with you; the inner sanctum of your heart lends credence for when a moment arises and you have stood the test of time you reflect back casting no doubt seeing the pattern of such vibrant blossom in your life. This is a foundation of trueness within you, a bitter sweet if you will, the story of a vast array of many titles, which creates a harmonious blend of spirit in life. Choosing a path in which to perceive the inevitable looking beyond the crimson tide of ill will or bad strides in life only generates a more positive feeding for the soul. Healing is a venture, a journalistic view from within which exudes the outpouring of, *yes, I will accept and move forward to diminish the improper surrounding my life to punctuate a purpose of understanding.* Acceptance is a big role in whole and in part that has traveled many stairways to heaven, thus leaving those with a glorified feeling of rejuvenation springing from the etched signs within the hallowed walls of one's heart.

Reach out and take the hand of the one who leads to all things good, for it is in you to accept the want to be cleansed and healed from any strife or any burden that lies among you. True love and devotion to yourself is a great practice to follow. You are number one; that is how God made you. This is the purpose of each of us and why we are who we are! Lifting your head high holding it there for all to see, be not afraid of what lies within your heart of hearts; it is best to unconditionally love yourself and love everything around you. Set yourself free, break the bondage of circumstance, foil the attempt of being captured by unwanted-ness for it is a lonely creature and we are not alone; God walks among you, living in you. Treasure your every breath while you cherish the moment in which you live for it is yours to have. God has granted this for each of us spiritually. Change what is changeable, fix that which is fixable, tend to the matters of the heart that need mending and leave every door open to you for your soul craves the passage of right; it belongs to you.

Look deep within your heart, feel your way around the positive-ness of everything you have, the insight or all spiritual saying to you I am and, yes, I will be. Never more torture or entertain the thought of negative-ness; begin a journey of your newfound freedom…healing!

Reflection, Awareness, Your Inner Soul

Does it ever hit a point in one's life where we stop reflecting or just a small glimpse of what is to either be a slight of hand maybe a twist of fate. Can it be something more than that we have instituted in our hearts and it grows in us to evaporate the ill will we receive?

The troubled souls or a road less traveled let's say that leads to a wonder of the woes of every thought we conceive needs answers to alleviate our inner strife. To regain what we once had in a sequence of events to literally cap the essence of none believing, we need to actually do reflection to gain from every moment captured. When we set out our soul for the journey of relinquishment of anything that we want a referendum for, we accept the purpose of wanting the right answers to make us whole again.

It's like the earnest child who wants the every moment of his mother for the comfort of his ability to receive her love; this is felt so deeply being conveyed in the purest of ways. Our souls beckon each time there is the need to refill that cup of life, to exasperate the truth of light feeling strong and whole again. The warmth we feel and the purpose it brings is the lightness in our hearts, which comes from what is right and our "right" to achieve in our everyday lives. If one grasps the strong hold of the light of spirit and feels the void being closed from the presence of love it is understandably a true Godsend.

We are and will always feel this with reflection, which enables one to become complete in every sense of the word. Isn't it good to feel the purpose of love a complete understanding for all wishing nothing better than a perfect day in this life? How grand a day it is when we obtain the truest form of light achieving for ourselves every aspect of meaning of life around us. Take a moment; look back at times that made you feel so happy. Capture that essence and hold it. This is it; don't let go. Realize what it is that brought you the simplest form of happiness relieving your inner self of the woes of every situation that brings you hardship, wrongful thinking, and even emotional strife. To every building block the foundation must be there for repose and resolve to everything in life that we cross. It's the actual acceptance we need to clarify with ourselves in order to move forward in life; we all have this road map built in our heart of hearts, our souls.

When a marital breakdown occurs one must ask why searching for answers but it seems both sides are too interested in pointing the blame at each other; this is being blinded by the wrongful thinking. Nevertheless it's the point of beginning and there is no real bad point or wrong point to start to reflect; it is the heart of it when you do start, which then will actually purify the soul. Start to look back at the purpose in life, why we met and how did we, what brought us to this point in this juncture that gave us so much peace before but now is lost? You will notice I said "we" and "us"; these are the key words to use in any transpiring aspect for soul searching for reflection. Search out that foundation you built the four cornerstones to that relationship seeking the rightful answers for your commentary. It's the togetherness the people need to see and hear the abundance of togetherness, the rightful ways of thinking that leads to an absolved crisis.

All of which is and can be rectified through reflection to what was the main goal in life. Another purpose is to find the fullness for the emptiness in one's life that "la dolce vita," the good life, if you will, the juice of life. Reflection gives every purpose for your soul in many aspects you will encounter as you strive for fulfillment and beyond. To search the records of time you have created and to sense the ever-growing purpose you are meant for is a true test in time. Look back at your life, look back with great love in your heart for you search the openings in life you created; see the achievements of everything made possible by you.

Remember you are number one and there is no one like you. The credence of everything you have and will be is in your heart of hearts; it pulsates to explode with love and understanding. You mean something in this life for you are counted and will remain a great purpose throughout forever in a day. The thought of knowing you means something; to an individual alone there is a galaxy of awaiting spiritual rising that will lift you higher than you have ever been lifted making the ground you walk on the foundation's cornerstone. You are that individual who matters most in this life, so take a look around, see what you bring in this life, touch it…feel it…see it; it's from you. Fill that void of doubt and bring a close to anything negative.

Reflection of anything gives purpose in one's life while it adds that so-called flavor...flavor to a dull and unsuspecting thought of I don't have any good intentions for my well-being. Exasperate every avenue, search out the real you, see the purpose, let it go. Anything that is ill will you can rid yourself of and accomplish many great things. The warmth you will recognize is just what any doctor orders; it will exude from you and others will notice. In turn you bring light to them giving a process of insurmountable acknowledgment to your heart. Open that window letting the sun in, as they say, let the warmth of the God-given day embrace you, lifting you up, for everything in life begins with you, and your, soul it has been given to you for a purpose.

To be aware of the attributes you bring forward to yourself and life in general is to cast no shadow of a doubt that spirit is there and you need to just reflect becoming a subtler acceptant individual. Remember this: *acceptance is the release of anything that binds you or is bound in your soul.* The true identification is the awareness you find during this process of reflection. The most divine acceptance you can do for oneself is to bring forth all you wish to rid and just do it, no inhibitions no delays. Do your heart of hearts a favor: accept. Awareness of all is the ability to self-heal, let's say, in the way of spirit is a right we all have. This can be accomplished with reflection, which is necessary to do every once in a while.

Once one becomes aware of the importance to reflect, it is a nature of the beast that it becomes second nature in itself. The way in which one will assume they are listening to voice of reason or the inner voice that lets us all know what is the truth behind the light is how we can be sure what is right when we reflect. Common sense tells you what is right and what is wrong (voice of reason) and your inner voice the spirit from within will do what is right in the light of spirit which always leads to a path of righteousness and good. The guidelines of morality are set in which we all recognize from day to day (voice of reason), the inner soul sets those apart from reason to what is perspective on light and spirituality.

The awareness of the differences also give great abundance of credibility to you and will help you achieve this goal in the light of spirit that you so much yearn for. The ability to turn around any situation through reflection is in your hands and in your heart of hearts, brings it out discover the true you that waits. For is it not true that *the warmth of all good deeds done lie in one's heart and to open them up releases good to all.* This is true for it is for you to discover.

Mountains can be moved with faith, hope, a complete understanding as tools, along with the reflection of good from within. The monumental task of achieving anything seems so small after you seek from your soul. Never give up on anything in life, for life never gives up on you. Everything in life begins with you; you are granted the love of understanding from our Heavenly Father. Reflection is a great way in order to gain a wholesome balance in life that alleviates the pain of today and tomorrow. The betterment of compassion comes from the never-ending cycle of events that we wish to glance upon, for it's within those channels we seek ourselves that very essence. To borrow a moment in time and hinge upon loving memories of loved ones or accounts of special occasions lifts one's heart higher with the urgency of belonging.

Feeling alone in life, abandoned from among your insight, never is it hard to turn a new page looking among the scenes played out over time and give yourself purposeful good will to move forward. The value of "you," in which is held in high regard, should always be glanced upon in retrospect giving high marks for all accomplishments in life, thus giving you the reflection of great love. Take heed to all that is given you in this life; respect it always, for it is the etched road map that lies deep within your inner soul that gives purpose to your life here. *Reflection, the way in which one tends to look for answers that will enable him/her to move forward and gain from any experience…Amen*

Chapter Four

Assurance of the Other Side

Learning to cope while seeking the proper resolve is but a road map that has many avenues to it and we sit in despair from time to time wondering what is the right course of action. We require, as humans, that one more antidotal prelude to what if's and how come's just to keep our sanity in any event. Take your heart, hold it in your spiritual hands and give it a tender little squeeze holding in place a loving spoonful of "right," which will take the edge off every discourse we travel through. Allow the very essence of your inner soul to grasp the strings of God's love, for it's in the re-assurance we build our foundation in us. Insurance in spirit is the assurance of tomorrow we so need!

To think of the way we are in this life and the things we search for day in, day out, the realization of every waking moment and then some. How profound is that thought to think about; it could lead you to begin to examine your own life in many ways that enlighten you more than you think. To actually have the conception of thought and the perseverance to keep looking beyond the realm of the now, towards what is realistic and true…spiritualism food of everyone. Grasping for the realism in spiritualism is in every one of us; thus we obtain unconditional understanding and compassion for the existence here and on the other side. Wouldn't it be a better understanding to say, *ok I want to know and I need that assurance of life, what the purpose of everything is and me?* Yes, it would and we have the right to express this in us and about us searching for that ultimate answer to every intriguing question.

Examining one's life in whole we see that from the time from our birth here we are always asking searching for answers. The re-assurance of life here, as we grow, needs perspective; thus through spirit it adds a different light to it and the other side. We become more intrigued and very consumed in the presence of spirit while beginning to feel the love and understanding we have been searching for that resonates in us, through us and all around us. It's like a rolling of thunder: when the sound cracks we get that urgency of wanting to know more becoming very aware of us and the fact we are spiritual beings.

The strength of spirit drives its heart in us giving us purpose; this is what we need as we seek those tough answers to why do things happen the way they do. Becoming assured of the other side is in us; it's like being home schooled once more for we did come here from there carrying that road map I always talk about.

Amazing isn't it to assume, hey how do you know this and how can I feel this? Well it's simple to explain and this is how I will explain it. That urgent feeling in your heart that yearns and feels so warm, strong like being invincible when you think of *home, is the* other side. Well that's how this carries to our souls and drives us to feel about everyone and everything. To be able to receive this feeling just look inside you; it's there. Look deep in your heart. Search the four corners of spirituality…compassion, understanding, faith, and truth. Seek what is yours, in you, and feel the realism in your heart. Caress it and hold it tight, for it is yours to experience; this is what God wants for all of us.

Deliver me from the pain in my heart. Show me the way. I want to be found. I need that directional guidance to assure me of what is the purpose of life. This continuous thought keeps coming up, and yes, we do require the answers, the insight to who we are or what is to become of our loved ones and us.

Think of this: you lose a loved one and you're in despair, stretching your imagination to the brink of nowhere. Then you start to seek the answers to calm the storm that brought the devastation to your heart. Every breath, every conception, every agonizing moment that passes you dig deep inside you pulling at those heart strings that make the ache in your belly hurt so bad. The pit of despair that sucks you in creates the biggest black hole that engulfs your feelings and every last bit of strength you have. This is what rips out your heart; it's the need and the want that takes over now. It becomes to you a quest to find the correct directional virtue to help you gain back your life. Remember to look in you, finding the ladder of hope. Let faith bring you out of that pit, that caged torment, which captured you making you a prisoner.

For all we go through we want the assurance of the other side, a little more explanation of what really goes on to bring us a calm and peace in our hearts. This comes in many different messages that are relayed many times over to us in vast, different, loving ways.

The story I am about to share with you illustrates this very way in which the other side comes through to us in a beautiful way. It starts on a morning chat session in the "Robbie Thomas Forums," a day I think many won't forget and, especially, Andy and Monica. "Lostsoul" is Andy's user nic in chat and he came in the room, as I was about to leave to take care of some business when I felt urgency for him to come back to the room later that afternoon. Funny thing too is he hasn't been in the room for a few months and it was very nice to see him, yet I couldn't place this feeling I was experiencing for I had other issues on my mind at the time. I explained to him to come back that we would catch up having a talk in the room later that day; he agreed as I took off for the morning.

When the afternoon arrived, I went back to chat in which I saw that Andy did come back as well. I started to pick up information for him about a Jenna name and much detailed substance to everything I was getting. During the barrage of answers and questions I had for him, he began to realize whom this was about; he then explained about Monica, how she buried her daughter that very day earlier. This had Andy upset and was emotionally overcome so I explained to him please have Monica call me. She lived the next town over from him so he agreed that he would right away. Monica calls me up within minutes to which I could feel her pain and loss, the torture of losing a daughter the very child she gave birth to. Monica was at peace hearing this for she received a gift from her daughter, one more time from the other side. As I go through information such as the street address and street name of Jenna, she was feeling her baby once more in her heart. Jenna even took me for a tour of her mom's home of great detail at which Monica was so happy to have this understanding of the other side being so close to her to allow her to reach out feeling her once more.

I do know whole-heartedly our loved ones come to not only to assure us but to put our hearts at ease as to the peace they have on the other side. Monica couldn't say much on the phone but she did validate every bit of that connection and it gave her heart the strength to smile upon a beautiful sunset for her daughter in heaven...God bless you, Jenna and Monica.

A few weeks later, I received yet another call from Monica, which proved to be miraculous in itself, as we spoke of Jenna and Monica's health condition. I had learned Monica was dealing with cancer and the doctors gave her a limited time if that to live. The miracle that was so astonishing was after the reading both Monica and I had with her daughter, Monica learned from her doctor that the tumors and cancerous cells were all but gone. This is a part of Monica I didn't pick up or let's say that Jenna didn't want me to. Monica couldn't contain herself; she was so happy very light in the heart and it was like talking to a kid in a candy store. She was so elated, for the news from her doctor was amazing. The doctor himself immediately booked Monica in the hospital for more testing, for he was totally taken back by the results. The doctor ordered further testing to Monica to see how her diagnosis is now the opposite of what they gave her.

69

I do believe that the fact of this connection from Jenna reaching out to Monica had created a beautiful spiritual existence within them both. There was a strong presence that day of the connection and as you will see in the reading itself you can feel it immensely.

®»»·†·ŠØÜL·‡·MÄÑ·†·««®: Andy who is Jean, gene to you forced the name of genie or Jeanie comes who in relation is this to you

«£õ§†§öû£» : soul were you talking to me

®»»·†·ŠØÜL·‡·MÄÑ·†·««®: yes I have that name lost and to me it is like in that area of close family relation

«£õ§†§öû£» : ummm no one I can think of... unless that is Monica's middle name ...or her daughters

®»»·†·ŠØÜL·‡·MÄÑ·†·««®: it becomes like a family thing and to me I felt like an aunt here maybe... I see like working in auto factory of sorts too...like something to do with auto parts here and right off it is a textile plant and I am in an industrial area and seeing this

«£õ§†§öû£» : sorry soul... maybe today I'm just not with it

®»»·†·ŠØÜL·‡·MÄÑ·†·««®: something too I am getting is someone actually looking right now for someone distant relative like trying to locate them but I have next town over... who do you know that was adopted out

«£õ§†§öû£» : I think it's April's aunt

®»»·†·ŠØÜL·‡·MÄÑ·†·««®: have you any insight to this, ok have her come in here if she will if she needs information

«£õ§†§öû£» : yes she has an auntie Jeannie

«£õ§†§öû£» : ok

®»»·†·ŠØÜL·‡·MÄÑ·†·««®: I will help her out but so far that is what I get and the funny thing is I feel like

70

I walked right past this person and its amazing the feeling was there but no words were said that close that's how I get this... yeah better to say come in and have a sit spell with me and I will do whatever it takes to help her

«£õ§†§öû£» : alright

®»»·†·ŠØÜL·‡·MÄÑ·†·««®: GOD BLESS ANDY

«£õ§†§öû£» : ty soul

Speed: too cool Andy

®»»·†·ŠØÜL·‡·MÄÑ·†·««®: no I think she will thank you, I think she needs this and has been looking there is something about adoption and looking... I get this too weird, but 16 *2 maple stone...maple something that comes

«£õ§†§öû£» : she's on the phone with Dr. right now... will call me back

®»»·†·ŠØÜL·‡·MÄÑ·†·««®: good a house that has a car in the drive way that isn't running this too comes to you it has some type of cover on it partial if not all... but it has a partial I see on it like its being worked on but not running this at all makes sense to you Andy... maple stone... maple ridge lane something like this

Speed: spirit sure threw a lot at you that time huh soul

®»»·†·ŠØÜL·‡·MÄÑ·†·««®: and house color would be like a white and a bit of very faint green like so soft like

«£õ§†§öû£» : ok... it has to do with Monica

®»»·†·ŠØÜL·‡·MÄÑ·†·««®: yeah really for some reason its time to get people together

«£õ§†§öû£» : Jenna was the name of her daughter that just passed away

®»»·†·ŠØÜL·‡·MÄÑ·†·««®: oh man really

«£õ§†§öû£» : Monica has an old 55 jeep in her drive way that doest run but wants to restore: her house is green with white trim I just called her but didn't want to say why I asked her

®»»·†·ŠØÜL·‡·MÄÑ·†·««®: what is her address street number

«£õ§†§öû£» : I'll call her now again

Speed: goose bumps I love the validation show

®»»·†·ŠØÜL·‡·MÄÑ·†·««®: it was as if I was shown this to let it out to bring people together

«£õ§†§öû£» : don't know how she'll take this.. Just got back from funeral

®»»·†·ŠØÜL·‡·MÄÑ·†·««®: oh boy well look wait... you confirmed a lot here

«£õ§†§öû£» : yes

®»»·†·ŠØÜL·‡·MÄÑ·†·««®: it's a lot we don't want to make her upset but let's say we hit it right on I do know this there is a message for her nevertheless

«£õ§†§öû£» : no... Although now she is going to want to know why I asked her those questions...I told her I'd call her back

®»»·†·ŠØÜL·‡·MÄÑ·†·««®: so this girl wants to and you to know she is around but is safe and sound and free from pain Andy

«£õ§†§öû£» : ok

®»»·†·ŠØÜL·‡·MÄÑ·†·««®: ok just say this to her what is your address say you're going to send her flowers something sorry to have to put you on the spot

«£õ§†§öû£» : ok... sounds good soul

Speed: must be cool to be u rob

Speed: I hope I become that strong someday

®»»·†·ŠØÜL·‡·MÄÑ·†·««®: no I am shocked I love people too much and care too much... I want her to know her daughter is ok

®»»·†·ŠØÜL·‡·MÄÑ·†·««®: but how now

«£õ§†§öû£» has left the conversation.

Speed: really

72

®»»·†·ŠØÜL·‡·MÄÑ·†·««®: she came in so fast Andy and for you hope he comes back… it was like this guys I am looking at her house and the color and the numbers and the street sign and then I see the car in the drive way not running and covered like I was being taken for a walk

Speed: he validated a lot but I would be interested to know about the house numbers… it's cool to me to watch these readings and validations

«£õ§†§öû£» : sorry got disconnected

®»»·†·ŠØÜL·‡·MÄÑ·†·««®: and he is here

«£õ§†§öû£» : more info

®»»·†·ŠØÜL·‡·MÄÑ·†·««®: oh sorry Andy go ahead

Speed: mercy Rob

«£õ§†§öû£» : address of daughter is 1682 maple street soul… you were right on !!!!!!!!!

®»»·†·ŠØÜL·‡·MÄÑ·†·««®: amazing… amazing Andy

Speed: wow

®»»·†·ŠØÜL·‡·MÄÑ·†·««®: did she start to question you

«£õ§†§öû£» : talking to her right now

Speed: imagine that Andy soul being right on!

«£õ§†§öû£» : lol

®»»·†·ŠØÜL·‡·MÄÑ·†·««®: is she ok

Speed: there's them dang goose bumps again

®»»·†·ŠØÜL·‡·MÄÑ·†·««®: lol speed… is she ok Andy

«£õ§†§öû£» : telling me about a dream she had of me her daughter and Monica: oh yes… I'll tell you of her dream… later

®»»·†·ŠØÜL·‡·MÄÑ·†·««®: can she call me if she likes

«£õ§†§öû£» : unbelievable

®»»·†·ŠØÜL·‡·MÄÑ·†·««®: I will love to talk to her about her daughter then if she likes 519 337 8333 office phone I am here

«£õ§†§öû£» : she said yes

®»»·†·ŠØÜL·‡·MÄÑ·†·««®: I would love to help her out any way I can

Speed: rob your blessings must rain down on you like a monsoon

«£õ§†§öû£» : she'll call you soon

Speed: and I spelled that wrong sure didn't excel in grammar did I?

«£õ§†§öû£» : ok off the phone with her now

®»»·†·ŠØÜL·‡·MÄÑ·†·««®: ok ty Andy I hope this helps her

®»»·†·ŠØÜL·‡·MÄÑ·†·««®: God Bless Andy

«£õ§†§öû£» : God Bless you too soul

After the connection Andy did sit with me a while to discuss Monica's dream and it only reinforced to him as well to her the fact that Jenna came through and it was supposed to be. It's a great feeling to be able to confirm for others the fact our loved ones are around us as you saw here. At a rate of just passing and they do come through regardless of time or distance spirit is free will. Spirit knows no boundary but the fact we are all tied and held together through love of God this is the unconditional quest of assurance we find.

Miracles do happen, and in this case, Monica not only was given a second chance to hear from her daughter with much validation, but the faith of assurance ran deep with the doctor's diagnosis being looked at once more. Monica stated she strongly feels her daughter gave her a second chance at life by coming to her through this connection and this makes anyone's heart reach out growing stronger in a great way. This is one very inspirational connection to the other side that shows each of us the true raw love and understanding that comes to us from our loved ones crossed over.

The main *assurance* as you saw here today is the fact the *insurance* that the other side validates to us through these types of readings. We never walk alone in life no matter how long our journey may seem in life here; we continue our lives on the other side fruitfully and progressively by always seeking to show unconditional love back to our loved ones in this life. We gain all our rights through our loved ones, which we all feel them in our own special way that validates us as well through the feeling of relatives around; we do succeed in the area of spirituality every day.

The compassion we see in the reading done for Monica and Andy does stress the purity of spirit, the willingness to reach out and acknowledge us here in this life exceedingly.

We all seek the realm of knowledge, a quest for information that goes beyond our wildest expectations, which drives us deeper into the pages of wanting, thus giving back to us the acquired vast knowledge of what we are and what purpose we stand for. The never-ending road that travels between this life and the life after shifts into high gear when one actually starts to feel and understand the essence of spirit in them. This gives you the truth that is laid in stone for everyone, the *right* we all share and deserve in this life given from God and Spirit.

Imagine yourself one day sitting there questioning everything you have come to know as faith, beliefs, the realm of spirit, then you take your hand, shake it at the heavens and gasp for the last breath you so desire to empty the dark feeling in your heart. You start to imagine the ugliness and unruliness that travels the anal halls of your mind becoming the exit of the never-ending story to a vast dwelling sorrow. Capture that feeling now; look at yourself in the mirror; think what am I doing, how can I go on like this, this isn't proper to exasperate myself this way. The validation or *assurance* of losing a loved one is so desperately needed that we sink to the far depths of despair clutching at every aspect to search our soul, seeking the *insurance* so desperately needed. We all feel the urgency to have this sign a true meaningful proper dialogue of, *yes, I can release all my inhibitions now and regardless of future endeavors of the same I can*

75

too still move forward and gain from this experience and have the knowledge to be "me" and love life and live it. The validations or *assurance* we all require is actually built in our own vast sea of love and soul, our heart of hearts. This knowledge does exist and coexist in us with our souls, which never leaves us but like a student being taught we need that affirmation of the afterlife; it becomes a great lesson learned.

There are many affirmations or confirmations of the other side and at each interval of every connection we all get grabbed, held tight from the love given and it does caress us so gingerly. In the connection you are about to see will illustrate how much our loved ones on the other side come through to assure us. The response letter to a great reading done for a dear friend of mine lends credence to the fact the other side gives us such pleasure knowing the assurance factor is built in our lives so clearly.

®»»·†·ŠØÜL·‡·MÄÑ·†·««®: Ame hon who has the Teresa name hon and I also have a William name wil …and for some reason I have making fun of the "w" name

Amethyst: Teresa is my aunt

®»»·†·ŠØÜL·‡·MÄÑ·†·««®: ok good I really feel I have to make fun of the w name

Amethyst: wil …ummmmm

®»»·†·ŠØÜL·‡·MÄÑ·†·««®: like either it was a joke or its someone they made fun of but it's like that with the W…Wil…William …loosing a nail here to

Amethyst: can't think of a w—got Johns and James

®»»·†·ŠØÜL·‡·MÄÑ·†·««®: something about losing my nail

Amethyst: Bernard lost a nail

®»»·†·ŠØÜL·‡·MÄÑ·†·««®: ok Bernard now he hit his self the nail I have like coming off

Amethyst: lol quite likely—his toenail has been removed

76

®»»·†·ŠØÜL·‡·MÄÑ·†·««®: ouch! Ok

Amethyst: the grandkids have jumped on it a few times too

®»»·†·ŠØÜL·‡·MÄÑ·†·««®: something that is not healing right it looks ugly lol

Amethyst: yes—he's been to specialists about it— it's a mess

®»»·†·ŠØÜL·‡·MÄÑ·†·««®: so now I go back to the "W"

Amethyst: lol—ok dead or alive

®»»·†·ŠØÜL·‡·MÄÑ·†·««®: so what does the W have here then...I see a number right

Amethyst: ok

®»»·†·ŠØÜL·‡·MÄÑ·†·««®: and it has many 3'S in it like I see 3 of them

®»»·†·ŠØÜL·‡·MÄÑ·†·««®: so what does 333 or the number 3 mean

Amethyst: lol...lol...omg

®»»·†·ŠØÜL·‡·MÄÑ·†·««®: oh boy what happened...lol

Amethyst: sorry catching breath here

®»»·†·ŠØÜL·‡·MÄÑ·†·««®: lol

Amethyst: crystal and I in numerology are 3's

®»»·†·ŠØÜL·‡·MÄÑ·†·««®: kewl

Amethyst: the last 3 houses crystal has lived in have been 3's... my caravan down south is 33

Crystallize has joined the conversation.

®»»·†·ŠØÜL·‡·MÄÑ·†·««®: crystal just in time... morning crystal

Crystallize: evening everyone

Amethyst: ((((crystal)))

®»»·†·ŠØÜL·‡·MÄÑ·†·««®: so this explains the number 333

Crystallize: in time for what

®»»·†·ŠØÜL·‡·MÄÑ·†·««®: all the three's

Amethyst: soul just asked what 3 meant to us

Crystallize: haha

Amethyst: lol

®»»·†·ŠØÜL·‡·MÄÑ·†·««®: stuck on the name though

Amethyst: who is William crystal...Wil

®»»·†·ŠØÜL·‡·MÄÑ·†·««®: I feel this person is being made fun of

Amethyst: soul picked up Bernard and his bad toe

®»»·†·ŠØÜL·‡·MÄÑ·†·««®: and that I am to make fun of this person something like this: William...will something like this: who can't plant anything for the life of them this is up too

Amethyst: our mother lol

®»»·†·ŠØÜL·‡·MÄÑ·†·««®: like not one green thumb on them

Amethyst: she kills houseplants plastic ones

®»»·†·ŠØÜL·‡·MÄÑ·†·««®: ok now this came loud and clear so it must be something connected to her the William wil or w name

Amethyst: help out crystal her father is john and brothers Charles and James

Crystallize: there's 4 Wilfred's on dad's side

Amethyst: oh yes duh

Crystallize: William

®»»·†·ŠØÜL·‡·MÄÑ·†·««®: ok so which Wil is I have that is I am to make fun of or you guys make fun of...who is the colorful one in like making fun of clothing and again stuck on wil

Amethyst: sorry I can't think of a single wil

Crystallize: it would be the one that hung around with dad

®»»·†·ŠØÜL·‡·MÄÑ·†·««®: flamboyant this is what I am getting here...so if Wilfred is the one you all made fun of or I am to make fun of, this is how it comes across

78

Amethyst: Yes I remember him mentioned—trouble makers together in their youth

®»»·†·ŠØÜL·‡·MÄÑ·†·««®: who is April 16 or the 16th and month of April

Amethyst: my daughter was born on April 16, on the 11th anniversary of me arriving in Aus and the our uncle died

®»»·†·ŠØÜL·‡·MÄÑ·†·««®: when I get this I get lots of flowers ok so there you go Ame...ok well the energy I have that gives me this is tied to you and all you have

Amethyst: wow

®»»·†·ŠØÜL·‡·MÄÑ·†·««®: the love that is sent is get here and very light so to show you he was here all you have is validated to you

Amethyst: he is remembered often

®»»·†·ŠØÜL·‡·MÄÑ·†·««®: lots of love to you both Ame and Crystal

®»»·†·ŠØÜL·‡·MÄÑ·†·««®: GOD BLESS YOU GUYS

Crystallize: kewl

Crystallize: you too

Amethyst: thank you so much

®»»·†·ŠØÜL·‡·MÄÑ·†·««®: you're so welcome

From: Sharon
Sent: August 14, 2004 5:30:43 AM To:
Robbie Thomas
Subject: Reading on 14 August 2004 for Amethyst and Crystal
Hi Robbie,

Thank you so much for the reading last night (your morning), it was really interesting and a lot of fun. After inserting the brain, a good night sleep and speaking with our mother, I can now validate a lot more of the reading. OK, from the top…Teresa is our aunt, on our mother's side, is alive and well and living in England.

We now know who "W" is. You were perfectly correct it is William. You heard correct. He is our mother's favorite uncle. The reason(s) we didn't know is that, 1: he died before we were born so we've never met & 2: he went by the name Bill so we didn't immediately catch on, though you would have thought we should have. Our Grandfather and William were brothers but they didn't speak to each together. William
& his wife (who is still alive, in her 90's) had no children and very week our grandfather would walk our mother down to their house so she could spend the day with them.

So William and our mother were very close. You said that you felt this person was being made fun of. Quite correct! As a child, he was treated in his family as being the stupid or simple one. He was always told that he couldn't have any dessert until he had eaten all his dinner. He would have dinner and then have a second serving, then find he didn't have room for dessert. This happened regularly and became a joke within the family.

Ok…losing the nail. Bernard is our father and a few months ago an ingrown toenail caused major problems. Wouldn't heal. He had to see specialists…it was a horrible mess and had to removed. Looking good now though.

The number 3… Sorry for losing it but it's almost a standard joke now…if you're making a decision on something and there is a 3 involved, you're on the right track. Crystal & I in numerology per birth date are 3's Crystals current house number is 3 but this is the 3rd consecutive house she has lived in that has been a 3. I have a caravan in a park down south and the site number is 33. We have 3 children between us. My house number is 13 and our parents 43. My work phone number starts 9333....

Our mother is the person without gardening skills...like I said—kills plastic indoor plants.

April 16...huge date in my life. Can understand why you got lots of flowers. April 16 1988...I arrived in Australia from New Zealand. (Crystal & I are Kiwis, not Aussies) 11 years later April 16 1999, in the morning our Uncle Charlie died and that very same afternoon, my daughter was born. Yes it has huge significance to me. I have to admit I hadn't been aware of the energy of Uncle Charlie around. When we first moved into the house we are currently in, we were inundated with visitors from the other side. Both my husband and myself were woken in the middle of the night with the noise of a party or gathering going on in our dining room. You could hear the hum of voices, people talking and the clink, "ting" of glasses. It never occurred to me that it might be Charlie...though when he was around, drinking was one of his favorite pastimes, so it makes sense.

You asked why you had been drawn to me so much in the recent week...2 readings, absolutely amazing and what this week meant to me....

"Ok don't be surprised Ame something happens this month special for you, you have knowledge of this or do you! Well to me it feels like someone or something from long ago coming through to you and will so in fashion of a big surprise."

On Monday, I spoke with a friend that I haven't spoken with for about 18 months; it was great to catch up. He was my first fiancé, I have known for 20 years, though we never married and went our separate ways

13 years ago, we remained friends. On Tuesday, it was my nieces 10th birthday. Yeah, just a major event. Now I don't know what Crystals excuse was, it's her daughter. On Thursday, the reason, excuse for me partying midweek and getting home after midnight, was a friend from New Zealand had emailed me to say he was over on business and wanted to catch up. We email a couple of times a year but I hadn't seen him in
17 years. LOL... I don't know if this is what you were referring to but it could well have been. Unless there is more to come and here am I going, nooooo nothing special happening.

Why all this connection to me so suddenly, I can only imagine my guides and dead relatives were having a bit of fun with me. A week or so ago Crystal & I were talking, after one of your readings and noting we had never had a reading with you. Our reasoning was that we didn't really need one.

Last week, you connected with Crystal, picking up that she wasn't well. A couple of the relatives, Alfred & Albert came thru then and validated with acknowledging the name plaque on Crystals house. That was so lovely. Then you had the connection with me during the week. Giving me a lovely run down on my life. It then turned into a reading about Crystal and her problems.

You are truly a very generous person. Thank you.

Thank you for the opportunity to a part of your realm, it is a wonderful space to be in. If any of this is ever of any use in one of your books, you are more than welcome to use it.

Thank you again for being a wonderful part of our lives.

Take care

Hugs

Amethyst & Crystal

82

From: Sharon
Sent: August 18, 2004 4:27:22 AM
To: Robbie Thomas
Subject: Reading on 14 August 2004 for Amethyst and Crystal (More Validation)

Hi Robbie

Got a bit more validation from your reading.

In the reading "William" had been determined to come through and connect.

As I said he was my mother's favorite uncle. His wife Lil is still alive in England.

I got a phone call from my mother this afternoon. She was speaking to England last night, to Lils sister. Lil passed away on Saturday morning. She was 94 and living with her sister who is 79.

I believe that is why Uncle Bill came through on Friday I guess he was trying to make sure he connected with mother, to let her know Lil would be safe.

As much as mother is a skeptic, she took this on board and when speaking with Lil's sister, told her of your reading. Lil's sister was thrilled. Said it was lovely and was so pleased they were together again. She could just see them sitting having a cup of tea together. LOL

Thank you. Through your wonderful gifts, you have made some people very happy and much more contented in the passing of a loved on.

Hugs

Amethyst

Through connections or validations as we have witnessed here we get the true sense of the other side showing us the ultimate in clearance and allowing us to grow spiritually in our search for answers of the beyond. It does give all of us a better balance of understanding of how much we are really looked after and the enormous insight to the unconditional love that comes pouring out from the other side.

Acceptance comes through in the next reading you're about to witness and enjoy. It gives the purpose of letting us know that we are still looked upon and cared for through intricate validity and very sequential moments. It becomes a great source of love that we are cared for so deeply and lends us all that vigor of life that we seek in the other side. We all tend to have the thirst of knowledge if you will, and that special moment craves us deep within our souls. The assurance of life after death is what every human being strives to find and some sort of sign to let us know indeed, is there life after death.

In the next reading you're about to witness it is very evident and thrown right in our faces with great joy. It gives credence to the fact we do not walk alone and, yes, we are also looked after from the other side. Relatives of ours always have a funny way of distinguishing properly little things that only we know and that gives the highlight of the connection.

®»»·†·ŠØÜL·‡·MÄÑ·†·««®: ok cinders hon ready for this

Cinder: yup

EnglishRose: I am lol…that's why I have been quiet lol

®»»·†·ŠØÜL·‡·MÄÑ·†·««®: you ask someone to come and to see if they will and for some reason I have a female and I get the name in two and sounds like to me Mary or Merriam

Cinder: my grandmother

®»»·†·ŠØÜL·‡·MÄÑ·†·««®: but I get both so what is her name

Cinder: Maria or English marry

®»»·†·ŠØÜL·‡·MÄÑ·†·««®: ok good now I don't want to jump the gun here but I have this too my

84

stomach is hurting and something to do with my stomach in relation to her this must be a sign of either stomach cancer or ulcers this is something of this
…vanilla is strong smelling to me right now

Cinder: I have an ulcer and IBS… she loved to bake

®»»·†·ŠØÜL·‡·MÄÑ·†·««®: October past that just past what is a mile stone or something about OCTOBER and this is for you too that comes I have two things an old picture of family gathering in black and white I see who married twice this is all close to you

Cinder: my mom and me

®»»·†·ŠØÜL·‡·MÄÑ·†·««®: this your mom's mom

Cinder: this is my mom's mom yes

®»»·†·ŠØÜL·‡·MÄÑ·†·««®: ok now for some reason a bureau

Cinder: my mom has stomach problems big time

®»»·†·ŠØÜL·‡·MÄÑ·†·««®: dresser I am to talk about hers was it

Cinder: yes…yes the pink one I use to shared it with her when I was a child

®»»·†·ŠØÜL·‡·MÄÑ·†·««®: I am getting so much on furniture things and paintings and items of such like then a word of auction to me something of the word of auction she acknowledges this and knowing of this

Cinder: the dining room suite yes my mom did yes mom had no choice

®»»·†·ŠØÜL·‡·MÄÑ·†·««®: nothing wrong I feel just she knows of this ok now since we on topic of family it has switched here I get sad feeling of this holidays of part of the family won't be together for differences set aside and if she was here it would be different …so to me I feel she was and still is the helm of the family

Cinder: yes she was

®»»·†·ŠØÜL·‡·MÄÑ·†·««®: ok hon number 3

comes up so this is a date the third and I actually get a time 11 30 am so the fact of time comes in is a significant thing and then I get a while we were on topic of birth this comes up so who born at 1130 on third of a date this is all close to you

Cinder: March would be my step dad...march =3

®»»·†·ŠØÜL·‡·MÄÑ·†·«®: ok what is the time that given me and birth related to it and who never got to go to opera, opera house something about opera

Cinder: me, believe it or not I like the operas

®»»·†·ŠØÜL·‡·MÄÑ·†·«®: you never got to go to see the opera were to go or something for to me it seems you missed out in this, this is acknowledged for you too

Cinder: yes...I miss my Nanny

®»»·†·ŠØÜL·‡·MÄÑ·†·«®: so she is giving you hugs hon and lots of ...stringing popcorn for tree

Cinder: this is her omg kool ty

®»»·†·ŠØÜL·‡·MÄÑ·†·«®: so what popcorn for tree is and meaning of a small tree a very small tree that's what I see too

®»»·†·ŠØÜL·‡·MÄÑ·†·«®: GOD BLESS YOU lots of love

Cinder: I have a small one up right now for my dani girl

®»»·†·ŠØÜL·‡·MÄÑ·†·«®: that shows you then she sees you

Cinder: yes

®»»·†·ŠØÜL·‡·MÄÑ·†·«®: lots to look at

Amethyst: awwww so sweet cinder

Cinder: ty Souls I so miss her

EnglishRose: awesome

Speed: good one rob

®»»·†·ŠØÜL·‡·MÄÑ·†·«®: she right there sweetie

Cinder: yes I feel spirits around just do not know who... ty Souls I appreciate this... yes I know

®»»·†·ŠØÜL·‡·MÄÑ·†·««®: happy for you you're so welcome

Cinder: ty ty ty Souls I was wishing to hear from her we use to string popcorn on the tree at home too when she was alive

®»»·†·ŠØÜL·‡·MÄÑ·†·««®: so kewl cinder

Cinder: dani was on me to put up the little tree on the table until I put up the big one

Cinder: so I did lol

®»»·†·ŠØÜL·‡·MÄÑ·†·««®: you have an amazing Christmas this year

EnglishRose: that is so awesome great connection soulie

Cinder: hiya thank you soul thank you so much

®»»·†·ŠØÜL·‡·MÄÑ·†·««®: your welcome hon GOD BLESS

Cinder: awesome Christmas

Once again a great connection with a great deal of validation that leaves one content with the assurance of the other side and the outcome. You will read her validation letter she sends me about this reading that furthers that validity of this connection for her. It is a pleasure to help individuals who seek the assurance, or "insurance," if you will, to the knowledge there is in fact life going on very much so on the other side.

From: Cindy Cinder
Sent : December 12, 2004 9:18:29 AM
To : Robbie Thomas

Hi Robbie

On Dec 8/04 I went to Robbie's room to chat, when Robbie said to me are you ready for this. I did not know what he meant at the time...lol, well he had a lady in spirit there for me. Someone he said, I have been hoping to hear from. This lady's name was Mary or Merriam he said. This was the lady I was wishing to hear from, my grandmother. Her name is Mary in English or (Mar e a) pronounced in Icelandic. Robbie went to tell me about someone with stomach problems he felt pain in the stomach. This is my mom who has this. I called her after and asked how her stomach was doing etc, she told me she was supposed to go for the Scope down the throat and she would not go. Well I told her Nanny came through Robbie to give you this message, stop being so stubborn and go and get it done. I did not know about this Scope test until I talked to her about her stomach probs. Thank you Robbie for letting me know!

Robbie went on to tell me about furniture being auctioned etc. My mom years ago fell on hard times and went into bankruptcy and lost everything and yes everything was auctioned off. My mom had no choice in this, My Nanny told Souls she was ok with it, felt like a relief! Then Robbie was asking about a bureau (dresser) that was hers, I said yes I have the pink bureau I shared with Nanny as a child, we shared a room when I was a child my Nanny was a cripple. Robbie asked me also about a number 3 and 11:30 birth time. Well the only one I know of 3 = March to me is my step dad not sure of his birth time though. Robbie then brought up who has been married twice and was shown a black and white photo of a family gathering; my mom and I both have been married twice. Robbie also went on to say, Nanny said if she was still here this would never happen, where part of the family would not gather for Christmas. Yes she was the one who held everyone together; yes there are rifts between the families right now! Souls went to say who never got to go to the Opera, well I said me, Nanny acknowledged that for him too. It was I. Robbie said, she is giving a lot of string popcorn to me right now, for a little tree; I just put up a little tree on the side table to do until we put up the large one. My Nanny and I use to string popcorn for the Christmas trees at home when she was alive. Robbie said, she is here and sees me. Just wanted to let me know that, Awesome, I know Spirits are around here at home just did not which ones came here!!! He says my Nanny's name has been handed down all I can say is, yes to this because my Mom's middle name is Mary and when my daughter was born I gave her the middle name Marie and meaning the same Mary in English, Cool Robbie Cool!!

Robbie you were right on with everything that my Nanny told you to relay to me. I thank you especially about my mom, needing the tests for her stomach. Nanny also told Robbie she is sending a lot of love to me, I miss her so and love her!!

I went back the next day to Rob's room to chat and said, to Souls and the people that were there, do u want to hear a story, They all sure, Well my Nanny passed in April 1977, Like I said we shared a room and the dresser (bureau) my side would always be messy her side always neat and tidy. After Nanny passed I would wake up in the morning my side or the whole dresser top would be neat and tidy. I thought at first who is cleaning this when I am sleeping? Well I would ask everyone in the house and everyone would say not me not me. I knew then Nanny, was still with me, cleaning the dresser

Then a few years after that I was sleeping and I awoke to see my Nanny at the end of the bed, we talked she told me she was ok and happy, then came this bright white light and poof she was gone!!!!

I just want to say Thank You Robbie for bringing my

Nanny through to tell me all this, especially about my mom and her stomach problems because my mom keeps things to herself, not to worry us. Well this needs to be looked at and I will get her there one way or another! That is also the story about the Bureau or (dresser) lol

Have a good day
Cindy

I was able to assist Cindy, in another reading when she entered the room one day. She seemed to have had an intruder take something of hers very valuable and things didn't seem right around the house. She was upset that day very much so I watched as she talked and vented a bit to a couple of people of the events that took place. I started to pick up on a few things and a couple of people involved, which ultimately more information seemed to fit right into her home and situation surrounding the matter. It seems someone entered her home as I explained; it was two individuals and one being the older of the two and one being the taller of the two. There were symptoms of one of chest infection-type thing along with breathing problems. The entire puzzle was coming very clear to her and she was taken back and felt very violated to the fact her home was invaded. As you will read her letter of thanks it illustrates the fact that spirit of our loved ones, guides or, yes, even angels do look out for us and we are presented opportunity for reprieve from wrongful doings. It was quite the shock for Cindy to learn the truth and when all was said and done happiness rang once more on her doorstep.

Here is the letter, Cindy writes to me, thanking me for helping her find the thieves and lost jewelry. It's one thing to be violated, but it's a great thing to have the "spiritual police" on your side as well. This day for Cindy she had that "spiritual police" on her side. We all pay witness to miracles in one's lifetime and for her she received two through both readings and she is blessed.

From: Cindy
Sent: November 9,2004 9:54:22 AM To:
Robbie Thomas
Subject: Thanks for the Help Robbie

Hi Robbie,

It was October 31/04; I went upstairs to get a gold cross and chain out of my jewelry bag for my son Ben, whose birthday is November 1. Each child received these from their aunt when they were born and I always give it to them when they turn 18. Well I go to my drawer my jewelry bag is gone! My husband even checked all my drawers, it was gone, nowhere to be found. I thought maybe, I put it somewhere else checked the whole house no way it was there. I was very upset but not mad, my heart was broken mainly because I could not give this to Ben now!

On November/04 I went into Robbie Thomas Forums Chat to talk and lift my spirits up. I told the story to everyone there, how my jewelry bag was missing and about Ben's gold cross and necklace was missing too.

I asked Robbie if he could help me, he started to tell me there were two people in my house with another son, when I was not there. It was not my son who took it but a tall boy who has a hard time to breath and coughs a lot. His father was with him, also the two were in on it. The jewelry was on a top shelf in a shed or garage type place, but the top shelf. I was shocked because I knew then which son and yes he did have two people in the house when I was not there. Plus the two people were a father and son. Robbie told me to be careful but that is where it is, and I would get it back, no worries. I thanked Robbie, I called that son and told him, I needed to talk to him right away very important.

91

I picked Adam up and told him my story! He was shocked and said, "I did not take your jewellery Mom!" I said I know your friends did. It is on a top shelf in a shed. He thought I was crazy but that is ok. The boy Darryl the son of the man has very bad Asthma and yes he coughs a lot. I took Adam back to my place, and Adam said, "I need to take a shower." I said, "Ok you still have clean clothes in your room." He needed socks, so I went to my room to check for socks for him, but something was nagging me to look in the drawer again, so I did! Low and behold there was my jewelers bag! The only two they're in the house with me that morning was my two sons Ben and Adam. I called my husband and told him it was there, well like hubby said, "it was not there yesterday I even checked for you!" I was able to give Ben his gold cross and necklace that day for his 18th birthday, which was a blessing. I thought everything was in the jewelers bag until I woke up the next day. I knew the Gold Butterfly Pendent was missing, but everything else was there. My heart ways heavy to know people in my own family you can't trust! I thank you Robbie for helping me to find the jewellery bag. To show me where to look for it and the people involved.

Robbie you were so right on with the help you gave me.

Blessings
Cindy

I am happy to have been able to assist Cindy in her plight to find the missing jewelry box, put an end to an unsolved crime that violated her family and their home. We all should take heed to the power of spirit, for we often think who is looking over our shoulder and my guess would be…the other side!

The next story I am about to tell you is a very inspiring one; it makes one think a bit. I was sitting in this person's home getting ready to give her and her daughter a reading when I started to feel to the back of me by the fire place a direct pull of energy. I started to explain to them that this room to the left of me is full of energy and something about the fireplace belongs to a woman who passed of chest cancer. Kim started to explain to me her grandmother passed of breast cancer, which confirmed to me I was being summoned by her to relay message to Kim and Michelle, Kim's daughter. Kim then started to explain that her picture was on the mantel above the fireplace closest to me where I sat. I started to explain that I know there is a celebration of a birthday coming very shortly at which point Kim spoke up and advised me it was hers, meaning Kim's in a few days. I started to get told to explain to take pictures on that very day and in the area in question. Kim then replied to me they have tons of pictures with nothing out of the ordinary on any picture before. I again reinforced what I was instructed to say and told her to take lots of pictures she is going to have a big surprise. We went on in the reading and validated quite a few things and now we were in the hunt for the pictures to come on Kim's birthday. Time passes and Kim comes wondering in the chat site and was so excited to say she had very much had a huge surprise caught on film while taking pictures in that room I suggested the activity would be. It was an "orb" fest on every picture she took, family and angels coming to celebrate her birthday. How amazing is that? She later posted in the Realm that it was the best birthday gift she could have gotten that actual assurance of the other side coming through in a reading then in film. I was so happy for Kim and her daughter Michelle to have had such an encounter that they will remember for the rest of their lives.

Assurance comes in many shapes and forms from the other side; some are so lucky to actually be invited to take part in a picture taking such as Kim and others through messages conveyed through connections. We are all truly blessed with the ability to be able to interact with the other side in such a way that we receive the assurance we seek and so desperately desire. *Assurance a stigma of hope and faith that runs deep within the walls of our heart of hearts...our souls!*

Chapter Five

Forgiveness

How does one find the peace in which they so deserve? One of the most sought-after answers yet never really sought thoroughly enough. The hindrances we so deeply horde within causes that meltdown emotionally and physically at times, but hey, what about spiritually? Keeping in check with reality is the most adequate start to any problem solving and your inner soul will not lie to you no matter how much you want a different outcome. Seek what is only righteous and see the proof. Take that carnival theme and let's trash it, throw away any circus thought that may enter your mindset shoveling the crap right out to pasture for nothing good grows from dead ground but dismay and disorder. Reach within finding that special person who has the equivalent of the want of forgiveness to actually give it as well. For everything in life that is given is reciprocated in same fashion, so to seek what is to do us well, let's set out on the wellness plan from spirit!

What Is Forgiveness?

Forgiveness allows one to release anything that has bound them or others in such a way their inner soul starts to take on burden and resentment leading to an inner conflict of them throughout duration of that individual's life span. Just the words, *I forgive* can absolve many problems for some clearing the air if you will of many undeniable hurt caused by oneself. To open up letting spirit in is to accept complete love and understanding of another to which lends credence to the fact we are a very forgiving society wanting to work in the light of *God*.

Harboring resentment only contains bad elements of the wrong types of spirit thus giving everyone involved ill feelings for long periods of time. This only establishes an unbreakable wall that does need to come tumbling down. Barriers that cause conflict are in many different ways all from not forgiving, thus containing hurt, resentment, hate, anger and sorrow all of which are so negative once one starts on that road they find themselves repeating that vicious cycle. All it takes is a warm heart, a spirit full of life, the openness to accept the love and understanding of forgiveness then watch those barriers start to fade leaving you with the pleasant feeling of, yes, I am free from this burden.

Hurt

The hurt we all have from time to time buried deep inside of us is placed there not only from the situation we are in but we allow it to take hold becoming that very institution that drives us crazy making us simulate everything we can imaginably think of to fuel the fire.

It harnesses us, becomes us and controls us leaving its mark of everything we don't wish that anyone would have to go through, yet again we are the *simpletons*, if you will, regarding the actual motion of letting this get to us.

We can actually take that negative energy turning it around releasing it then capture the proper understanding that it does not control or harness us. We are very much alive with spirit that will uplift any individual that accepts forgiveness.

Resentment

When one sits pondering the point of resentment they think, *yes, I am caught in this web I have weaved; I would love to be able to extinguish it moving forward but how to do that it is just too hard to contemplate,* so I stay mad and in the end resentment eats away at the very soul you tried to make well again.

Being scared to take the first steps to actually acquire the thought of *forgiving* is only going to keep one unsatisfied while still searching for answers to those impeding questions *why, now what*, and so on.

It's like taking those first important steps as a child: we need reassuring in making our first move. As too, we need help on the road to recovery and in order to obtain that assurance we first off have to make that first step towards self-love a self-agreement thus leading to the words that we all hope to have *I forgive.*

Feelings of resentment again only contain all negativity a big time waster. Living life to its full extent like there was no tomorrow is what we should all reflect to in order to establish the foundation of life's little secrets that enables us to move forward.

Hate

In becoming to this point and it's a very strong point to be in, we have let ourselves become the situation that has evolved in us. Letting oneself go to this point is also letting one's inner spirit and the meaning of spirit elude them. The compilation of every emotion we entangle ourselves in drives deep in us, hence we get the opposite of forgiveness in every meaning of the word.

For one to come to this point we must also become the hate that drives us to this point, so isn't it fair to say we create every aspect of the meaning of hate? To analyze this word and to accept its meaning would only defeat any purpose to resolve any matter whatsoever.

The turning point of any complicated situation is acceptance and reflecting toward a better outcome for all involved. To take your inner soul crushing it beyond repair is not in any of us; we are of *God* and we desire to be full of spirit. There is an outlet of relief for any situation; it's up to every individual to accept the point of forgiveness. It's been instilled in us from the beginning of time. Turning the page allowing a new script to be written is a great step towards fulfillment and happiness.

Anger

The amount of energy that goes into this very word is exhausting; it leaves one thinking only once again the negativity it brings and not so much the lighter side of life. It disables and not enables one to move forward. It will create a vast dark hole if you will that will engulf anything that crosses its path.

You become entangled in such a way you can't see straight, think right or even function properly on a day-to-day basis because you're so involved in this dark area, which ends up eating the very existence of your soul.

One has to examine the parameters of life that is set, not only by us but by what *God* would want us to live by. We have to look deep inside and ask the question, *Do I want to be like this?* That alone will start off the exact counter effectiveness everyone desires to move on and gain the light of spirit.

We are the ones in charge of our lives with every preliminary thought, action and, yes, every emotion is in our hands. We control it; we are able to turn things around containing and rid ourselves of negativity to absorb the light of *God*.

Sorrow

This is one emotion we have experienced in a lifetime more than we care to admit. Like a roller coaster ride we go up and we go down only to become swallowed in that very arena of sadness that leaves each and every one of us sunk in the depths of despair.

Here is how we rise to the occasion defending ourselves against these elements of distraction in our lives. To cease on the action of letting one get that low beyond the point of no return we again have the controls right in front of us. They are in us; they are us.

Assume responsibility for one's actions is up to each and every individual. To be able to instill this in your heart, let go of negativity, let it drain out of you, think positive always and remember *you're number one*.

If we always allow every aspect of any situation to take hold of our very soul and burden us with sorrow we will never move forward.

and I am going to make the betterment of this
r your soul to grow stronger. This also allows the
art of hearts.

_ ....ve the right to do as we wish in life, offering what we
want in life, but wouldn't it be more practical to do well in every
aspect of life and what it has to offer us. In every mention of the word
self-control we do have and we can exert to every corner of our lives the
necessity that enables one to gain fruitfulness of life in spirit of *God*.

Forgiveness, the cornerstone to life's solved problems. A Ferris
wheel that travels only in one direction to the betterment of every
individual here in this life and is so easily obtainable we are the key to
every success of the very word. Just to say those very words once again
enables an individual to become fuller, more prosperous in spirit and
gives the proper perspective in what life is all about. The one most
selfless act we can have for one another is to be able to have in one's
heart the compassion for this very institute of forgiveness. It brings
everyone closer to the realization of spirit in us all. To have the quest for
the knowledge that brings us to the very steps of joining together
and alleviating that one problem, the little hurdle of forgiveness,
it will enrich one's soul brightening any spirit.

Take a moment reflecting back to a situation in your life that had
cause for forgiveness, then look back even further and see the length of
time in which it was obtained. You will see the amount of time that was
wasted in the thought of harboring that hardened centerpiece that lay
in your heart called ill feelings and the sense of lost spirit.

While we examine this situation we also get the sense of relief
knowing we are over it putting it behind us. It does not control us nor
are we affected by that situation anymore. What was it that brought us
to this point? Was it obtainable through our hearts accepting and
forgiving? The answer is yes, we feel better knowing we were able to
distract our very soul to enable ourselves to grow in spirit. Now if we
can take a page out of every lesson we have learned, use it as the pillar to
which we stand by, we would be able to move more effectively
toward the light of *God* allowing more easily our ability to forgive.

Forgiveness comes from within us, to be able to establish one's love and understanding for life or others we have to be able to first look deep inside seeking the first signs of forgiving. We must do a check of our very inner soul saying to ourselves, *I forgive me, I forgive me.* This enables the first steps to a recovery program that everyone goes through and don't even know it half the time.

To allow oneself to become whole again while initiating any procedure towards self-forgiveness only enables that person to seek more outside attention giving the forgiveness to cross over falling onto any situation they are involved in. It all starts with you; every aspect of forgiveness always starts with the one who is holding the key. We all can do this by releasing all that negativity and reducing our own heartfelt subdued passion of ill will. To move forward we have to draw a line in the sand making every mention to the fact we are going full out relieving ourselves of this situation we are involved in that makes us retain that very thing we just spoke about, *ill will.*

Sometimes we harbor feelings we have that are of self-guilt, driven by an outside source that takes us to a level we need to assure ourselves we are on the right steps to forgiveness. We search for that mystical way out or if there is any glimpse of hope for restitute of resolve. Trying to rationalize with anything that pops in one's mind, to either overanalyze or even depict the outcome in different circumstance. Bargaining or substituting anything less than looking for forgiveness within will lead to an unfortunate vicious cycle once again.

Release those inhibitions of guilt and ill feelings; then look outwards offering the same. It allows one to begin the absolute in every sense of the meaning forgiving. Take upon yourself to reach out searching that avenue; letting go is a great way to fasten you to spirit becoming whole again in the light of *God*. Conquering our fears of not being accepted in the light of forgiveness or not accepting in our own hearts the fact we forgive is not intended to do well. If one opens up within accepting both in their heart and soul the light of forgiveness towards others and themselves, this will allow them to definitely conquer that element.

The exact fulfillment came true for one lady I was reading one day in the chat room. We were brought together in the arena of forgiveness. A sure sign of love and understanding was bestowed upon her in this great connection from life on the other side. Melissa regained the strength through communication and forgiveness. She has started to move forward in life as the lady we connected to had established for her, bear witness to this incredible truth of love and understanding.

Añg®¥§ñåï£: soul... I got a Q. hope you can help

®»»·†·ŠØÜL·‡·MÄÑ·†·««®: sure try

Åñg®¥§ñåï£: my step mum got an angel card reading it said there was a message from a passed love one it didn't say which one.

®»»·†·ŠØÜL·‡·MÄÑ·†·««®: right

Åñg®¥§ñåï£: oh hang on she is abusing me

®»»·†·ŠØÜL·‡·MÄÑ·†·««®: you want to know

Åñg®¥§ñåï£: for asking you lol

®»»·†·ŠØÜL·‡·MÄÑ·†·««®: oh you're getting it now you're getting abused by her now.... lol

EnglishRose: lol...

Åñg®¥§ñåï£: yes lol

®»»·†·ŠØÜL·‡·MÄÑ·†·««®: well lets wait a while and see how much she abuses you then I might answer...lol

EnglishRose: Mum leaves snail alone lol

Åñg®¥§ñåï£: she is like "Bel, why are you asking?! It doesn't matter. Don't bother this poor man!"

®»»·†·ŠØÜL·‡·MÄÑ·†·««®: lol

EnglishRose: lol

Åñg®¥§ñåï£: my mum is so silly sometimes

®»»·†·ŠØÜL·‡·MÄÑ·†·««®: who was sister to her I feel like a sister to her in a way its a lady energy to her and when you talk about that I get it to me like that

Åñg®¥§ñåï£: asking her...hang on.

100

®»»·†·ŠØÜL·‡·MÄÑ·†·««®: for some reason too my chest hurts here to snail hon so its related to that and this person my right side more so than anything

Åñg®¥§ñåï£: she is hmming me

®»»·†·ŠØÜL·‡·MÄÑ·†·««®: snail hon who passes from either cancer in the chest area and its close to her and I feel like sister feeling here like on same level

Åñg®¥§ñåï£: she is talking cryptically to me lol…hang on

®»»·†·ŠØÜL·‡·MÄÑ·†·««®: that's whom I am feeling at present here when we talk

Åñg®¥§ñåï£: ok.

®»»·†·ŠØÜL·‡·MÄÑ·†·««®: snail hon something too about angel or angels and to me its something she would know about this is from her like this she should know about

Åñg®¥§ñåï£: yep, asking her…she has someone in mind

Åñg®¥§ñåï£: good work lol

®»»·†·ŠØÜL·‡·MÄÑ·†·««®: ok

®»»·†·ŠØÜL·‡·MÄÑ·†·««®: lol

Åñg®¥§ñåï£: omg… she has finally worked out who you are talking about lol

®»»·†·ŠØÜL·‡·MÄÑ·†·««®: now this April coming is something too the month of April and also I have November here two months being acknowledged here something about the number 5 it comes after the months, what does rose petals mean to her I have that too like I am laying down rose petals for some reason sprinkling them…yes it does I see it and its like sprinkling down of rose petals

Åñg®¥§ñåï£: SNAILS MUM: "we planted a rose for Shaun's mum but I also have roses on the poem I wrote for the other person"

®»»·†·ŠØÜL·‡·MÄÑ·†·««®: for a reason though this is an acknowledgement of that

Åñg®¥§ñåï£: yes.

®»»·†·ŠØÜL·‡·MÄÑ·†·««®: angel or angels and its all tied here

Åñg®¥§ñåï£: Her ex's mum said she would always watch out for her…she died of throat cancer.

®»»·†·ŠØÜL·‡·MÄÑ·†·««®: and this is the person we are talking about I have the cancer on my right chest area like it spread obviously then that's what I had

Åñg®¥§ñåï£: ok. She is a bit confused… That's why she is taking so long to answer.

®»»·†·ŠØÜL·‡·MÄÑ·†·««®: so the person we are talking about the one close to her like a sister would be her

Åñg®¥§ñåï£: yes.

®»»·†·ŠØÜL·‡·MÄÑ·†·««®: good that's how I get this for her the things so graphic here today illustrate that she is around her and know about her poem and the angel thing

Åñg®¥§ñåï£: the poem thing was for someone else.

®»»·†·ŠØÜL·‡·MÄÑ·†·««®: it's here though that's what I get about the rose petals

Åñg®¥§ñåï£: mum said there is nothing in April, but on the 30th of March.

®»»·†·ŠØÜL·‡·MÄÑ·†·««®: November here too and the number 5 comes in here to snail what happens on the 30th

Åñg®¥§ñåï£: it's a bit touchy that subject

®»»·†·ŠØÜL·‡·MÄÑ·†·««®: someone passes and buried in April

Åñg®¥§ñåï£: yeah well, I'm guessing so!

®»»·†·ŠØÜL·‡·MÄÑ·†·««®: right so April is what I have here hon the month of April…so now what about November and funny thing again the number 5

Åñg®¥§ñåï£: soul, can I invite you into my conversation with mum?

®»»·†·ŠØÜL·‡·MÄÑ·†·««®: yes hon sure can

After joining Lorna along with her mother in a private messenger chat, more was learned to the fact of the car accident and the guilt she felt over this for years. She held this deep in her heart all these years, which she was looking for that assurance or a message if you will from the other side to let go, something tangible in essence of a big sign of forgiveness. The validation of many things we talked about, that was her sign of relief. In fact there were too many incredible remarkable validations that did come through for her; it was a sign from the heavens that she needed.

While in discussion with her, she walked me through the whole part of her life that was actually touched by this devastation of loss of life and how she coped with it. I explained, *we control everything in life around us and more important we have the control for forgiveness*. I explained she need not hold on to this anymore; she was forgiven. For it's not measured in the amount of time but how your heart opens up accepting the love and understanding unconditionally.

The energy in that conversation you could feel was so strong. The actual *act of forgiveness* she was discovering while opening up realizing to love life and live life. You will now bear witness to the extreme love, an understanding that took place after we went to a private chat forum. Here is when we came back to the main chat room and the heartfelt words of those close to her.

Åñg®¥§ñåï£: does anyone know what an amazing person Robbie Thomas is?

Amethyst: yes but confirm it for us

Winged: yep we know

Åñg®¥§ñåï£: give me a sec amethyst

Skyy: yes we do and we are all blessed just to know him

Åñg®¥§ñåï£: my mum has been holding so much guilt inside from an accident she had a long time ago and soul is reassuring her and I can feel the weight being lifted off her shoulders

Skyy: good that's great

Amethyst: so sweet

®»»·†·ŠØÜL·‡·MÄÑ·†·««®: back… one sec guys

Åñg®¥§ñåï£: wb soul (((HUGE HUGS))))

®»»·†·ŠØÜL·‡·MÄÑ·†·««®: ty

Skyy: wb soul

®»»·†·ŠØÜL·‡·MÄÑ·†·««®: I will ask snail if I can tell you guys this had a great meaning behind it big message you have to see it ok I will tell you see the woman and the rose petals

Åñg®¥§ñåï£: go ahead soul

®»»·†·ŠØÜL·‡·MÄÑ·†·««®: well she wrote a poem right about roses and a while back she hit someone in a car accident when she was 5 months pregnant and that lady ended up passing over but then I had a male come and this fellow I described and all to her it was for her too

Åñg®¥§ñåï£: the woman was high on prescription meds and alcohol and walked across a 6-lane highway

®»»·†·ŠØÜL·‡·MÄÑ·†·««®: he was very not happy in life here

®»»·†·ŠØÜL·‡·MÄÑ·†·««®: so when we look at the reason for her to write that poem and light a candle al these years for that lady the release of the rose petals and the fact of that male coming through too to show he was unhappy showed two things her unhappiness and the other side of forgiveness…she can let go now she can move on the lady came through to show that

Amethyst: beautiful

Skyy: yes that is

®»»·†·ŠØÜL·‡·MÄÑ·†·««®: big message here she was torn up inside over that and she needed to be told and we got the message…AMEN

Winged: amazing job soul

Åñg®¥§ñåï£: ((((((soul)))))))

Skyy: yes it was

®»»·†·ŠØÜL·‡·MÄÑ·†·««®: ty

From: Melissa
Sent: March 8, 2004 4:10:15 PM To:
Robbie Thomas
Subject: Forgiveness Connection

I just wanted the thank you Robbie for passing on the message of forgiveness to me on the 4th of March when we talked...

It took a while for me to connect things that you were telling me, but as they say "the penny finally dropped."

You picked up on a ladies energy and the months April and November: on the 30th of March I was driving home from a family gathering when I struck a lady who was disorientated and stepped in front of me. She died and I have blamed myself for it ever since.

You also picked up the number 5 and it having something to do with a passing or a birth, this took me some time to figure out as well but then I realized I was
5 months pregnant with my 3rd child when I had the accident. You also picked up the sprinkling of rose petals or something to do with rose petals: I write poetry and had written a poem in memory of the lady which I put red roses and buds around the boarder.

As you said I have carried the guilt of this accident and the ladies loss of life for coming up six years now and it was a great relief when you gave me the message: there is no need to hold on it is time for healing and forgiveness. The sprinkling of rose petals, release it. You told me that she knows and said, "believe me you are forgiven."

WOW, what a huge difference it has made to hear someone else confirm and to see the words written "you are forgiven." I have taken the poem off the wall every year since and lit a candle in front of the frame in her memory. This year I have decided to do it one more time and also sprinkle some rose petals, I will attach the poem I wrote her to this letter so you can read it.

Words are not enough to express how this has made me feel, but I know that you understand what I can't say in words. Thank you so much and I look forward to talking with you more in the future.

GOD BLESS YOU
TAKE CARE
Melissa

PS this is the poem I wrote
In Memory of Leila 30-3-97
I wouldn't have known you if we met in the street But
I guess it was destiny that our paths should meet I
wish it had been different how our lives crossed
I would have preferred your life wasn't lost
I'll get over the shock well I'll do my best
I pray you've found peace now you're at rest
I can't change what happened it's now in the past
But the memory of you in my life will last

I am so happy for Melissa to be able to move on, to actually open her heart up and forgive herself of this tragedy. Even more so having the blessing of the lady that was accidentally killed by this car accident. The reassurance of this, *live life and love life,* most certainly takes a page out of that book and transcends it tenfold forward to us all as a reminder, that we have the opportunity to forgive.

Holding on to one's hurt or any other emotion that involves not being able to forgive oneself or another surely *builds walls and barriers.* Therefore we need to understand more about the concept of forgiveness. In doing so, we graduate to a higher level of learning.

In the series of forgiveness signs if you will, one travels through a dimension of many untouched waters that cover a whole area of emotions that directly intercede giving comfort after recognition of the fact; we need this in our lives in order to grow. The spirit of one grows stronger and learns lessons to which everything in life has purpose in that fragment of a moment when we realize the effectiveness of the words, "I am forgiven" or " I forgive." We will start to reach out and accept love and understanding more readily.

I had the opportunity to read for a lady that has been visiting "Robbie Thomas Forums" for a while, which we had a connection that was easily validated with many interesting facts. Her grandmother was killed in a car accident involving a train shortly after leaving her place some time ago. She came through just after the anniversary of her death on the twenty-third of February and the actual accident date being the tenth of February. It wasn't but a few weeks later I was feeling this strange energy around Lorna and she too was complaining of having a strange feeling as well. All this hinged on her father's death just within days of both her and I receiving these strange emotions. It seemed that no matter what felt, we both were pulled in directions that we couldn't put our fingers on it. After her father's passing she took some time off then decided to venture back to the "Robbie Thomas Forums" for comfort and to see her friends. It wasn't but a few moments she entered the room, when her friend Elton began to surface bringing a big smile to her face. He (Elton) began to show me things so I was relaying them to her left and right. What a character and a good friend of hers, he came to her need and was there to help her through a rough time.

The actual signs of forgiveness come from Lorna's letters she wrote back about these connections it is in great detail. She does share with us all how forgiveness takes hold of your heart regardless, enabling one to grow stronger in faith and spirit.

Dear Robbie,

You contacted my beloved friend, who passed away last year. I knew a reading was going to start last time he did one for me he got a bloody nose, this time he said how he was having a hard time typing. Yet, I thought the reading was for someone else. Took me around 5– 10 minutes to understand it was for me .He wanted to know who I called mannered. I laughed so hard. My friend I called him that, as in a dork in a way he was just always annoying me on purpose he liked to see me get riled a lot said I was cute when I got upset. His cat was also named mannered. We had a kind of relationship that never needed words. We often finished each other's sentences and thoughts .I lost a part of me when he died. He was very open minded and never judged regardless of how crazy my thoughts where that alone was peaceful and relaxing. I've missed him like crazy and think I will forever. He has never left me in spirit in all that time or do I feel he ever will. That has helped me this last year but also caused some confusion as to what if I was holding him here and therefore not releasing him to go on a live in heaven. Robbie reassured me that was not the case. Phew was that a relief. He also mentioned a joke Elton I called him AL and I had since we have known each other (3–27) was about a body part. Elton preferred girls with a more voluptuous body frame or so I thought know I think that was another think to get me riled up another thing to get me ticked .I believe he contacted Robbie today to inform me that   though I am going through my hard time emotionally right now it was a reminder that I am not doing it alone as I have felt.

Thanks Robbie for all that you are and all that you do.

Love always Lorna

Lorna really takes that leap in her next letter that really explains all that one can desire in the words of forgiveness, the actual letting go and learning the lessons of life. Lorna then writes and also

108

witnesses her own transformation from holding on to all that emotion of a vicious cycle that really takes one for a loop in the mindset of feelings that control us and our very spirit. She takes control and adversity has no bearing any longer in her life, which it enables not only for her to grow but enables her to learn more about herself spiritually.

I must admit the amount of time and the time span that her connections took place were so inviting and at a most appropriate time they were. It is a great pleasure to have been able to not only help Lorna but also in doing so everyone who witnessed this also in some retrospect grasped the love and understanding from it in every fathomable way.

From: Lorna
Sent: March 29, 2004 1:17:18 PM
To: Robbie Thomas
Subject: Validation Response

Personal experience of forgiveness I had to find within myself. Growing up for me was a horrible experience. I was part of the child abuse, and witness to physical fights between my parents. I lived in fear of waiting for the next outburst to happen. Alcohol and abuse was the norm for our household .We assumed this was what happened in all families. My brother, sister and I were all placed in foster homes after my sister tried to commit suicide. When she arrived at the hospital, there was my mother's handprint across her face in a welt. That was the beginning of our new life. I was 12 years old before the state finally took us out of the environment. After years of being in a foster home I vowed to myself I would never put myself in that situation again. I would never allow a man to hit me, nor my children. Alcohol would not be a norm but an occasion. Holidays have always been the worst for me and I still have nightmares from the past.

Every day was a constant battle. I have anger and pain in me that was taught. I am always comparing myself to them, making sure I do not end up like them, is one of my biggest fears. June of 2003, my sister called to inform me our parents were both in the hospital. We were informed our parents went on a drinking binge for 2 weeks straight. The adventure cost my father a stroke as well as being permanently paralyzed. My mother had a nervous breakdown and was having heart murmurs. All of three of us children showed up at the hospital to see what needed to be done. Here was a man I hadn't seen in over 15 years, whom I had so much hatred for. I couldn't bare it .I tried to see what all I could do for him. . I hate to see anyone in pain and that he was. I did my best and went home. That weekend was the hardest one to face in all my life. I had to finally accept all that was in the past that I had carefully ignored and blocked. I called my uncle who has always been a mentor to me as well as a father figure. What he said to me pretty much sums it up. He told me baby girl, their good people who never have all their children present when you need them the most. Who can't find the time to be worried enough to be there, and here you all three were there. He also said "Honey you have to let go of this anger the only one it is hurting is you." I thought all weekend on those words and realized I just couldn't let it go. I decided for me it was time to ignore and leave the whole situation alone. During my time away my mother finally stopped drinking and started living. My father was sent to a nursing home to be taken care of.

From being paralyzed, he also lost most of his brain functions. He was that of a 6-year-old child mentally. He barely spoke, couldn't read and had a hard time remembering the names of everyday household items. Also some time during his treatment developed gangrene in his right leg, therefore had to have his right leg from knee to foot amputated. Since June I thought of this as his judgment time .I didn't see him living much longer but he had to face all the wrongs he did. On March 16th 2004 I received a call informing me my mother was sent to ICU. He developed a bladder infection that went into pneumonia. Due to him being diabetic, the doctor and nurse informed my mother they do not see him living much longer and to get there as quickly as possible. She received her call at 10:00 a.m. us children made arrangements, arrived at the hospital at 3:00 p.m. I looked at my father, he was ghost white, cold to the touch, tubes everywhere, eyes staring above him. The hospital cut off all circulation to all body parts except the major organs he needed which was the brain, the heart and lungs.

He couldn't blink his eyes instead he had to have artificial tear dropped put in regularly. I saw him and new not only he wasn't feeling any pain but he was barely living .All day long I watched him die slowly in front of my eyes. It is horrible. I saw his skin turn three sizes from his normal; I witnessed his skin take on the purple hue. At 10:15 I couldn't take anymore. I couldn't understand what it was he was waiting on. I just wanted it over I wanted the agony to stop. I finally shut the door of the room .My brother and I was the only ones present at the time. I touched his arm and said to him "Dad, this is Lorna. I am not sure why you are hanging on but please let go now. I thought about it all day and I just couldn't tell you I forgive you. I can't accept the hell you shown the life or us you given us. Yet what I will accept is you were the way you were to show up what it was we didn't want to be, through our experience we learned what it is we want most for ourselves. It is time for you to go now .No more pain please. Accept god now." No sooner I told him how I felt the door burst open telling my brother to get the rest of the family now. He died as they opened the door to his room. Everyone was crying including myself. It was such a hard emotional day. I cried that night when I got home questioned what kind of person I could be if I couldn't even bring comfort to someone who was dying and feared I cost him to choose the other door .I cried and prayed I never heard my children to say those words to me .The next few days was hard as well. Our parents we not wealthy had no arrangements for death. Us three children had to not only make the arrangements but also find a way to pay for 12,000.00 for him to be buried. We all knew it was our responsibility. Yes he didn't care if we were provided for and he wasn't a good man or father but we still knew we had to do it .We felt anger towards him and my mother for putting us in the situation, pain from our own mother not even being able to say thank you. Yet we prepared and buried him in taste. The funeral home was phenomenal, huge, and elegant with a touch of class and comfort all in one. The day we arrived at the funeral home, I walked into the room with my best friend, the first emotion we felt was guilt. Here he was no longer living and I could feel his guilt. That was an eye opener to me .My uncles words came back to me "honey the only one you are hurting is yourself." He was right. I learned not only do we harm ourselves with not letting go but also we are not able to move forward. I also hated the thought of anyone moving on feeling pain or guilt. Regardless of what type of father he was, his judgment on his self is much harder than I could ever feel. I walked up to the casket, looked at him and told him .I forgive you now .It is time for you to accept the light and god. From that moment forward I have felt lightness to myself to my emotions and defiantly to my heart. I have peace now because I was finally able to forgive .I realize now I had to say what I said as harsh as it was as mean as it was I had to say that to finally be able to accept.

I thank you Robbie for helping me out so very much, you are truly a blessing and this I will never forget.

God Bless You,
Lorna

For every turn in life we come upon many obstacles that need a bit more attention and that being said we all have in us the power to look a bit more carefully at the words of forgiveness. It is in us to give and to receive, live life fully enjoying each day given us sharing with everyone. Forgiveness allows us the strength to move forward not only with life but also within each of us. It's in you, remember this always.

Chapter Six

Burden on Our Souls

Having a heavy heart laden with wrongful intentions leads one to the road of despair. We travel this road looking for compensation of any sort to compromise our own feelings. Does one really have to give up what is purely the right way of thinking or feeling to enable the trust of making burden leave us? No one has to cascade any thought of rendering any intention of misplacing our own true inner feelings of our soul to gain any lacking of true moral existence in life. Search inward and all tools to repair any discourse or ill intentions set upon ourselves from indulging in the factual events of taking on burden lie inside our heart of hearts...our souls. Offer up today to God the burden of what will be tomorrow's new quest to seek answers and write a new script in the process of positive attributes of you. Take not upon yourself, which you would not put there, and give not to others the same, for it's better to have a shoulder to lean on rather than carry the weight of burden!

When we sit and let anything derived from ill will or ill intentions bind itself to us, we set up a premise for burden. The trademark for this is simply the wrongful insight to a grander way of enlightenment. Anything you lay between the right and the wrong path of directional virtues requires more in-depth analysis to stay afloat in perspective properties of living spiritually. Everything we do is earmarked in our souls, which entails great perception on our parts to see to it that burden does not become the discourse of our lives. The heaviness we sometimes feel can be alleviated through proper feelings and enlightenment of our souls. Walking the righteous path cannot only be thought of but has to be implemented along the way, opening each gate while stepping through to the next proposed situation that causes grief. Burden is the absence of anything *rightfully* acquainted to us spiritually. Becoming the pillar of resistance, our heart of hearts strengthens each time we recognize the torturous thoughts of that selfish trend.

Accompany nothing that is relevant to malice or should you acquire the distaste for such propaganda, this is just a precursor to self-destruction, which disables and not enables your spiritual growth. Justify your actions through your vision of what is proper in the light of everything moral; disregard the intentions of undesirable discontent. The reverence of all-good comes from within and not from sources of laymen fascinations that become the distance between truth and untruths. Search out the abyss of disheartened analogies and take the picturesque theatrics, discarding them to the recyclable virtue of understanding. To search the improper dimensional fortitude of ill will only give way to more disheartened bad taste that is cumbersome to your soul. Reason within, seek the truth among the annals of despair, and lay in stone the proper thought of recovery to allow the essence of all to shine through.

If one allows the ridicule of every judgmental aspect of another or another's actions to sit heavy on the wall of burden, it builds a tremendous amount of weight that becomes the cynic of nothing more than a hurtful birthmark of hate and anger. Traveling the road of the vicious cycle of hate and anger the frustrations build; we become over endowed in that testament of what lies beneath us. When this ugliness rears its head, tranquility of your soul should be reflected upon to set the stage of betterment and the proper channels of dissolving the ridicule that plagues you. Do not hesitate to stress this to yourself for it is in your soul to be free of such dismay upon the truth of enlightenment you seek.

Your inner voice follows what is truthful and the pre-notion of all aspects of proper conduct is in you; it's the road map to integrity and the abundance of respect for all. Keep looking for all good out of all bad while seeking everything that is the morality conscious meter, for it keeps tabs on everything presented throughout life. The precursor to improper thought only leads to an equivocal response from your soul, expressing disregard for the circumstance for which you are entangled. We all know the feeling of this and we have traveled this road many times; it becomes the never-ending story to bewilderment and settles in your stomach like a heavy rock. Don't consume what doesn't taste well, and only chew what you wish to taste, for if we actually do bite off more than we desire it also engulfs us draining the aspects of feeling whole.

Expression of falsehood, which stays with you like the markings of a scar, becomes the flesh-eating machine of spirit. Covering actions to save face or attempt to shade the truth is only but a bad handshake with a destiny of fathomable discontent within. Knowing the wrong behind the curtain of sight is exactly the mirror image of discourse you feel while the words or thoughts slip across your tongue. Before the thought of, *misguidedness* enters your mindset put the roadblocks that distract the entertainment of anything less. The thoughts that pool around or stew beyond belief that give recognition to despair and troublesome feelings, make them bookends for the lessons are in between the lines of fortitude you will find. Shed not a hope or the faith required to banish ill will for the love of spirit burns a flame inside your heart, which lights the way for you and all. Deceits of any sort only plague the true bindings of moral respect and spirituality, giving a bitter taste in one's mouth. To become rid of this distasteful happening and the occurrence of it ever taking shape, reflection of true self or the preservation of enlightenment within shines deeply to overshadow the wrongfulness. Don't fall prey to misconceptions that might intrigue you or step into the midst of mystic bad happenings; it only lends credence to the fact digging a hole keeps getting deeper. Telling non-truthful wordings will leave one tongue tied and burdened with guilt for it concretely solidifies ill will. If we examine the faltering of us, the inner sanctum of us becomes decayed with the perspective of going, *why do I feel this way and how would I rid myself of this burden on my soul?* Be not a statistic to yourself or anyone else for that matter. Fester none of what deceit may offer; bring always good to the table of life.

Self-pity is a grand way of burden laying markings on our hearts, which in turn grabs hold of our soul lowering us to an unveiling of sadness and depression. Let not the flagrant obvious take position among your proper thinking; stay true to the course of what is right and seize every moment to seek justification of being well in spirit. Do not lend an open hand or invite a problematic situation to take abundance within. Show more stamina for spirit and yourself by opening up accepting all that is good. Create the happiness within by shredding the negativity that is the ball and chain holding you bound. Spirituality is a great source of vitamins that entail all the nutrients needed to have more perspective in your life, thus tending to your inner soul and nurturing it gives the balance needed to grow. Look not upon the distaste in life or the blackened eye you may have acquired but look inside pulling out those proper tools to love and understand yourself. Reach inside; find the resilience and reserve the emplacement of spirit. Levy not what you want to be the recourse but place the heart of all-good as the forefront. Start to tear down those walls of self-pity, for they only become the decay of burdened waste. You need not destroy your thoughts of angelic good; it's a part of you always. Faith is embedded deep within you; hope inspires you and determination drives you. Always look forward and never back, for we stand in a moment in time and we need to continue to step to the next to grow. Choose your path precisely and accurately; let not the road of self-pity cross your way and shut your eyes to deception of any thought. Remember to always keep an open mind to everything positive; those that travel the road of negativity only burden themselves with darkened avenues. Examine the prospects of reality and search only tangible thoughts of *truth* to resolve a matter of feeling displaced. Spirituality is the enlightenment to the truth of everything we are; seek the truth and hold the sword of justice for it is yours to have.

It may seem these times are contagious when we think that the hours is passing and there is nothing left here for us to grow despite the relentless nagging prospects of eternal peace but how to accomplish this. Is there a cure among us, from the weakening of our thoughts of no point of return? Yes, finding the memories of reflection and spirituality is all laid in the road map we have etched in us. Despite everything one feels and thinks of the negativity of an end to a means the light still shines through and we then have to learn to take that pity we feel and shed it; become stronger enabling our ability of spirituality to flourish through and through. Burden that lies on our shoulders from this self-made distraction is a fixable one at best, bring out that person that screams to be heard and seen. Give the truth of the matter a chance, a real chance to feel stronger with each day that dawns.

Loathing is a burden of our soul as well; this creates a premise of seeing ourselves better than another, which in the end we are all equal by every standard in life. Gathering up steam going nowhere is the perfect description of this; it builds the character of nonsense and at most a jail you keep yourself entangled in. Who gives one the right to challenge or shelter the thoughts of unwillingness to set free the equality of each human being (spiritual being), not one man alive has the right to begin to fertilize any such inkling of such a thought. This only creates the burden that has represented much in the way of slavery to one's soul. The boundaries of such shouldn't be breached or tempted, setting yourself up for a grand fall in a spectacular way you are. Spirituality has no home for this type of unwillingness that carries the burden of self-destruction. Burden has many faces and to keep piling up one after another only creates the black hole of uncertainty. Indulging in retrospect of a circumstance while feeling the purpose serves you properly is a misguided influential mistake. It's better to actually admit the fault we have and try to correct it by looking through that which has created us to feel so heavy within our hearts, thus giving us the proper loving understanding we all seek. Spirituality gives this purpose in life for all lending that magical moment of relief that allows our hearts room to breathe.

Equality in life is the shared experience for all and all benefit from such truth, which makes everything crystal clear. A good thing to do in this circumstance is to actually seek the refuge of spirit from within, be not afraid to let spirit into your heart; you will be surprised at the response you find from your soul. Gather no moss for a true self that is true to you is the whole purpose that nothing has a tie too but love of spirit. Complicating the world we live in is something we all do very well, leaving us the suffering and anguish, if you will, to sort out when we sit pondering the point of why me. Giving us that chance to leave every open door available to us, which we need, will create the purpose to seek resolve. Reach down deep inside; don't be a statistic in the evaluation of reference but rather become the ever-sought spiritual being you are.

Pride is everything that will end up killing the purpose of life within an individual. The wisdom that underlay the thought of *accommodating self-indulgence in the circle of life* renders nothing but a strong sense of burden that piles up in heaps. Gathering of self-respect is a necessity and not the other of pride. Search within your soul seeking what is needed to replace this guilt-ridden prospect of utter worthlessness. To keep one in suspended torture of becoming prideful and in thought of such is a very vague way to be in life. Take it upon yourself always to reflect back and give thanks for what we have in life, thus releasing burden and anything to do with burden to God.

Why wear a crown that bears the resemblance of pride, for no one becomes king of this domain; it carries the bitterness of self-destruction. The cross is too heavy to bear; let the burden go and create a happiness that acquaints itself with the proper love and understanding we all desire. In the end all will become such a load on one; the effort will always seem so tiring to most and thus lessons are a hard way to travel. Walk the road less traveled and seek only what is enlightening to your soul; burden in this area is such a pain it brings many to their knees wanting answers for the its so blinding they can't see the truth.

Envy a destructive feeling of burden that leaves one wanting, in doing so the want outweighs the need. This is such a self-taught desire that controls the essence of what is proper for an individual. We get so complacent in the home of envy the air that surrounds us is so vial, leaving us gasping for the want of everything that we need not embellish our souls to. Why embark on a trek of this sort for it begins the end of everything spiritual one seeks? To want or to desire of which another has generates the burden on our souls and a cavity of despair. All around you weakness has made much, a poison, a thorn in your side; break that bond between this gross neglect of slumber in your soul and wake to a better you. A perfect picture is the one that includes *you as a whole individual not separated from faith and ho*pe. The substitute of your needs from reality to the wants and desires of imaginative compromise only leaves you empty inside. Fill that soul's heart with the complete understanding of compassion and love for all, especially you. No more wanting, for everything you envy now is all but a myth and you have made a prelude to what is the just in life, giving your soul a burden free absolute. Envy is a very destructive way to crash through lessons in life, leaving the equation of how to fend for the spirit in us. Spirituality is made of the four cornerstones, which evaluate compassion, understanding, truth and faith. This is all absent from envy, encompass you around those elements and become much more driven in spirit.

The falsehood of lesser than what you feel you are is just that; never think otherwise for *you are the greatest gift God has given*; your life means so much more. Do not take in account the things you envy, for it destroys a great virtue in you. Things in life are acquired through all you do and have become in this life so seek out what is the truth for you. Take the time to heal and mend your inner self; give the fighting chance and lose the envious ways so readily obtained; they are but a bad habit. Look upon others, see their situations and wish them well, *for all good come to those who are most loving of others*. Do not give up or become weary of anything in life; envy gives one this and it leads to a dead end in the end so keep your head up and always look to the light of spirit.

Consuming oneself in the partial or in whole of the realm of greed is a banishment of spirit in any sense. This only provides the burden of our souls with anguish over what is morally right, distressing every thought of the truth and all rightful intentions. Setting a footing for a crumbling foundation leading us astray to a malice place of unwanted-ness, which sounds like a rotten recipe? Who can be complacent or have any solace through this epilogue of events that play over and over like a broken record inciting a hardened heart. Self-portrait that has many different faces to it is an unfinished picture with no end in sight. Playing out a role of king of the hill trying to knock off any purity of spirit that thrives only of good is but a little mound of dirt that is easily swept away in time. Becoming a circumstantial point in life will give you the tedious trend to fend for the liberty of honor and equality falls short in this story line.

Who wants to be trend setting anyways and who wishes to be set aside for another day knowing that greed has finally befallen a different path now? It's funny how the faces of burden rear themselves to us; they serve no purpose and are but the insult to life. Search the very essence of what you were when you entered this life, bare for the world to see and naked to the truth, thus the innocence of everything that was, will indeed surface once more. Serve nothing of greed for greed serves itself and is a very lonely sacrifice among much good. Spirituality holds no home for this type of conscious action for it only destroys the very work set by God. If one wishes to be consumed by this, why not try being greedy and serve spirit? In turn do something proper to say you have fulfilled the very essence of you. Turn the tables: become extraordinarily happy and in being greedy you can also share in the light of spirit...*now that's something to greed over*.

Jealousy is a contagious element of burden that seeks a prize of emptiness, nothing left to the soul but hardship. It's a long way to run if it's an uphill battle, finding the solace among the cure for sanity is a prescription definitely quested for. The world may revolve around a different direction in this plight and gives off bad energy that attracts negativity at its best. Trail blazing in the absence of spirituality leads to a crossroad of an undesirable caution scene. Crossing the line is actually the exit to the very introduction of spirit and the pleasantness among your soul. Understanding the things that drives us to torment in burden is titled but footnotes of depressing afterthoughts of *Where do I go now?* To pin blame for a subject well studied as we grow in life is nothing more than subjecting you to more obtainable sequential bad habits of burden.

Being in the fray of jealousy and the home of ill will is the emptiest position to be attracted too. Empty that shelf of rotten text leaving the bookends to fend for themselves. Jealousy is a monastic venue at best, giving off the array of pungent recourse of hurt and resentment. The silence created by noise stirs the echoes in the walls of the burning aftermath of nothingness. Shelter yourself from the devastation discovered in the hallowed precursor to the truth of the meaning of sharing among your fellow man. Relieve your innermost fears while accomplishing the most satisfying feeling there is when you accept the very essence of spirit. The truth lies between acceptance as well as the willingness to convey and relay good will. Jealousy is the unhappiness that shares the home of all burdens without the resolve of the innocence. Hesitation compounds a momentary refrain of your insight, which leads to the signs of nothing left to sustain a joyful spiritual being. Gathering up the intuition of spirit while belonging to a beginning of resolve births an innocence of life shedding that trend of overbearing adversity.

Ignorance plays on one-heart strings and the chorus is always changing never keeping beat or time leading one to a dismal, frail repertoire. Clouds of thought seem to plunder all around an individual, blinding them from seeking the propriety of feeling good about themselves. Having so much hate, that is the acid in the core of one's life, only produces the yearning for betterment. To cast the shadow of distaste, one must be aquatinted with the buffet of indulgence of selfishness. This is one of the most distracting burdens that has so much repetitive unfortunate circumstances that follows a river that runs deep with agony. Feeling quite weak in the prime of anyone's life throughout, shadows feelings of torment and disgrace which paints a series of ugly intentions within one's heart.

Take the simpleton out of the simplest fragment of madness that screams and beckons for hope and faith. Give that reprieve that is so much desired to satisfy the urgency of belonging and feeling refreshed with spirit. Tear down the thorns and razor wire you have set up; exclude yourself from the ever-hindering problematic burden surfacing in ignorance. Begin the steps to the road of recovery through spiritual means taking the garbage out for the last time.

The forthcoming events have taken place in people's lives and the biggest burden of all is the fact denial sets in so rapidly there is no time to blanket it with understanding. If one becomes so caught up in the moment of surrender thus venturing out in the wilderness of misconceptions and undeniable denial, what is there left? Going fishing are we, to an ocean of emptiness that waits with a whirlpool of deception. How many fathoms lie between the bottom of this seabed of burden that has no shelter from storm. Denial is the worst concept among any instructional advice one can give themselves. Be more honest to yourself and open to the truth for if your door is open good will comes. Keep in mind that you only seem to fool one individual with this burden and that is you. Take heed to the concept of change and address it accordingly; it may save you a lot of heartache.

Burden is the heaviest of life's torments; it seems to stick to you, which it feels like the never-ending story of sadness. Take a moment to pause and reflect to every aspect of your life searching for the very plot of the story that you need resolve from. Continue your trek to find whatever it is the soul searching you are doing requires. Give yourself the data to work with and absorb all fundamental truths that will bring you together with your soul once more. Never give up or never say no, for the truth lies within your heart of hearts…your soul. Burden is grand wastes of time; don't get caught up in the mess of unmentionables as these subjects we touched upon here. Fight back in spirit with the complete love for understanding of spirituality. It's in you to say you're number one; seek the truth finding the help required. Ask your guides and angels to show you. Ask God to take the burden from you. Prayer is a great way to start the day or the ending of the day's events.

Give thanks for what you have, and begin anew with the love for yourself. Reflection of good is the perfect way to express the ultimate unconditional love for spirit and your soul. Lift that weight off your shoulders; release it to the universe, which God is ever seeing to all. Feel good inside and always think positive for *only good things come of positive thinking*. Forgiveness is the ultimate in sacrifice. Do yourself a big favor and forgive you...amen

> I seek refuge among my ruins,
> This fallacy of nothingness surrounds me,
> Of what do I learn if one is blinded without sight?
> Torture me no more,
> Leave my side pungent distress, The
> seed of everlasting does dwell,
> Procrastinate no reluctance in me,
> For now blossom is in full bloom,
> I grow to be all I can...Amen
> ...Robbie Thomas

Chapter Seven

Most Commonly Asked Questions

If one never seeks answers how does one accept the outcome or even derive a thought to purge beyond the norm. Set your sights upon high; ask every available thought to conjure up questionable outcomes and place forward or in motion the questions that so desire proper evaluation for your soul. For every great teacher there is, that teacher first had to be a great pupil, in doing so had to listen and then asked many questions to seek the inevitable. We all are placed in life to quest the purpose of life, while doing so we evaluate the sequential events laid before us in our lives. There is no right or wrong question in life; never be afraid to question spirit, for if we do we are in check and our faith is always there. Question the day you stop asking; then look inward and ask again. There are many answers to life's questions; we are all pupils in a learning mode!

In the essence of the will to know or want to know we find ourselves at the helm of a great quest for knowledge, endless searching for our right path to walk. We all sit and ponder points of interest throughout our lifetime; a vast section of it is questions that lead us to various answers and opinions that at best either leave us bewildered or at some kind of agreement with. *Knowledge is a great*

surmountable collection of data or inner love that we gain through life and it reflects in the way we all exude from within. The course of right or wrong is neither a correct way to establish the parameters of setting up house for the astronomical amount of understanding we acquire in this life. To fulfill one's hunger to divulge amounts of interest, we all require the right frame of mind and inner understanding to carry the right correspondence to a higher level of learning. Assume we gather our intrigue in the manner we gather the warmth we hold in our hearts for spirituality and we put the two together, what a combination to have. When we have great aspirations to feel need for knowledge in anything in life, be it spirituality your daily activities or anything in relation to an individual we care about, we always have our right intentions set forth.

There is no set requirement really only the great willingness to learn and love of understanding that comes from within. This chapter is based on the total questioning of many individuals over the years and was given great thought of before rendering it feasible to use. It gives great pleasure to share in these many questions and answers that will I hope lend a great earmarked understanding for you as it has for me growing into the light of spirit over many years of my life.

Q. Why does God take our loved ones so young in age or even babies from us? What type of lesson is this?

A. Throughout life we all have various trials and tribulations that we deal with on many different set terms and conditions we set on ourselves in order to come to a realization of what may be the right answer. In this type of question we seek the truth of the heart and in answering it properly is that God calls home his children when he sees fit and the lesson may be one of whatever length of time we have in this life with our loved ones is of a pure love for us for if it were a long life versus a short life. It is never easy to let go of our loved ones in any ordeal we may have been going through but it's one of the hardest questions to answer, for no one man nor woman alive can stand in front of God and completely answer it. The only truth behind it is we are given many choices in life and we are *spiritual beings having a humanistic experience* and in order to grow we have our trials and tribulations; thus we have a quest for knowledge.

Q. Finding my abilities how or which is the best way to determine how I can achieve this?

A. Whenever we have that deep gut feeling of truth, understanding, compassion and faith, we reach down and are touched by this; we are given this overwhelming feeling of inner strength deep inside us. We begin to actually have that sense of, *spirit touch*; one is empathy, which each and every one of us do obtain in this life from life on the other side. Hindsight 20/20 well its intuitional values we carry to know better in every step in spirituality and guides us further in life. We all have ability and it's up to each to be *accepting* to this, which enables each to grow in spirituality, and therefore if we seek each door will be opened for us. A great way to practice your ability is to actually write down encounters and keep a log book or journal to reflect back upon; this enables you to see the progression of which you crave. Writing down your daily activities through spirituality is a diary of your events; this gives you time to review your notes and to keep perfect record by having dated materials.

Q. I hear a voice just as I am in a very light sleep, just drifting off and I will hear this and it startles me for it either calls my name or is saying something to me! What is this?

A. I have given many different examples of this over the years to which all explain that our inner self reaches out to us frequently to let us know we are very aware of us. Now your probably saying you agree or you're mystified by this. Well it's true we often dream correct and during our dreams we have many encounters. Well same holds true for us in travel, *astral travel*. This is done in many ways, not just one singular sense, for nothing in spirit is singular or on a one thread to say. We are reminded that we are given ourselves a wakeup call, so to speak, to say hi I am here and inside you. Spirit is ever busy and that special spirit in you is very busy as well; your inner soul is reaching out to you and saying hello making you aware. So next time you hear a voice calling your name and you're in a very light sleep and you wake up wide eyed wondering what the heck, don't get all worried for you're just saying hi to you.

Q. I feel like I am cursed and that someone has sent demons to me. I have nothing but bad luck. Is this true?

A. The only (bad luck or demons) that you have or even a curse be it so, is that, *you let the power of suggestion of another influence you.* This really never gives you authentic proof or validation other than you're going nuts worrying about it being true. No one person can curse you or send demons to your doorstep to do their bidding; this is not a movie from which we get delusional or let our brains weave patterns of many ill-willed thoughts. The only true spirit is from God, done in a fashion of good and in the name of God. If you think about it, *we would all walk around saying boy, I wish my ex-girlfriend or my ex-boyfriend or whoever for that matter, that their hair would fall out and her toenails curl up and go brown!* Wouldn't this be a freaky world we live in then! It's just not true or reality. Thus this puts this question to rest along with all that Hollywood horrific thought patterns.

Q. I feel I am from another time and I have such love for that certain time in which I feel so strong for. I have thoughts of it and dream of it, flashbacks, and I was wondering is this possible?

A. This holds true to many of us for we all have reincarnated, and a reincarnate will experience such feelings like being drawn to a certain time or era, place or even objects. The sense of belonging to another or even a visual that leaves us yearning to be that once more goes through our very soul from time to time. We are drawn for a reason and this reason is in the pit of our stomachs put there for us to remember who we were once before. We may feel a strong love for a loved one we left behind during a time in which we crossed over then to return to this life, which is like a record put in our very soul and bookmarked. If you have such feelings of this, *I strongly urge you to keep record of any visual or feelings you receive,* logging them, and while this collects for you in time you can reflect getting a better understanding of you and who you were once long ago.

Q. When I dream I have a hard time remembering things. What is the best way to do so?

A. A great source for you is to keep your very own dream journal. Have it handy close by so that, if you remember finer points, you can always jot them in reviewing what you have. A dream journal is an excellent record of achievement, as well for it holds your messages you seek from these encounters you have. Once you have established a great sense of ability to write in your thoughts and then to actually review them, then you are able to even go a bit further determining what the message can hold for you. Dreams are a great array of messages that our sub-conscious delivers reminders if you will to settle unresolved issues at hand. A dream journal lets you express your most inner thoughts from your sub-conscious, and hey, what a way to actually stay in contact with your inner soul!

Q. How do I know my loved ones are around me and is it them I feel when I sit alone sometimes? It's like I get these feelings of being watched but it's a comfortable feeling.

A. Our loved ones visit us often. When I say often, it's on a regular basis to look over us and help us out in times of need or just to signal they are close at hand. Those feelings you discover are feelings of intuition. Never doubt that, for it is instilled into your heart of hearts, your soul, before coming here. We all have a draw to our family members, our loved ones, and when we have such feelings of being looked after or sensing them close by, then you are actually using your intuition to do so. Our spirits do more than just sit in the temple upon which God gave you; we are very active indeed in this life. Part of that activity is sensing and accomplishing your ability to feel our loved ones. So the next time you have such feelings of these, remember, *reach a bit deeper and see who it is or reflect back: did you call upon them to visit you in your time of need?* A simple way to answer this also would be, *you do the same for them, would you come to their needs if roles were reversed...you bet you would!*

Q. Orbs or lights on film in my house or pictures I have taken around my family activities what are they?

A. This is a good question! People often mistake this for just spirits but not just any ordinary spirits, no. See, for these orbs of light or flashes of light are angels or relatives that you have captured on film. Loved ones who guide us or send love to us constantly always surround us and we have angels our guides that are amongst us as well. Sometimes you may capture them on film, while other times not, but when you do it's a great way to say hello to you and a very good shot to keep. Orbs of light are nothing that can harm you or you have no need to fear them for they are again just around to ensure and assure us of the other side. It's a special time if you capture orbs on film in and around your family members here in this life for it sheds light on the subject are we alone or not!

Q. Meditation, what is it and does it actually help in spirituality?

A. Meditation is a great way to learn to relax and obtain patience in the virtue of seeking answers relying on your intuition. There are many types of meditation and we can examine them here right now. Watching television, listening to the radio are great ways to release the reality world escaping for a brief moment, thus giving you a time away from the then and now. Daydreaming, here is one great source of meditating, for say 2 minutes or less is a great way to also say hello to a different way of relaxation creating the premise for escape. Then there is the actual mediation; this gives us a great lengthy time out to find our inner peace becoming one with the universe while releasing all negative energy and absorb the positive-ness spirit has to offer. Meditation is a great medicine, if you will, *a natural prescription that will heal the inner soul and mend many fences*, if you give yourself a chance to learn. This will enable you to open up more be more accepting and thus creating again a great sense of intuition of spirit in spirituality.

Q. What is an earthbound spirit and what can we do to help them? A.

An earthbound spirit is one that is trapped between this life and the next. They become trapped for such reason could be a thing of which they died a horrible death and are trapped for the suffering they are enduring not knowing how to cross over. It could be that they actually are stuck here searching for a loved one not knowing they have passed over as well. They see us as occupiers of their home or land. Confused at what is going on this creates a sense of bewilderment for them. To help them we should encourage them to seek the White Light of God and to accept his love. Talking to them, explaining that we all love them and express it sincerely while explaining that their loved ones await them on the other side. Positive energy will react positive to you so to show faith, compassion, understanding and the truth you have the four cornerstones to spirituality and you can guide them home.

Q. Healing our souls, is it necessary, and what can I do to progress to heal myself?

A. Our souls are above all the energy in which God has given us the, *birthright* to spirituality. It is in us to maintain and create a happy home per se for our spirit. In doing so we create a happy home for ourselves in this life. *Healing is drawing positive energies from everything around you that is of love, pure love, and turning that into a reaction for your soul to grow.* A great way to heal is to write out your aspirations, all-positive, then take a look at what you have written down for yourself acting on that one item at a time. Prayer is a great way to heal, and asking for blessings while expressing blessings to others, this gives your heart a chance to open up accepting things we cannot change but can move forward to a betterment of our souls. These are but a few ways in which we can give ourselves that chance to reach out and heal.

Q. What is déjà vu and why do I get feelings of things happening before?

A. Déjà vu is a normal process in which everyone deals with in the normalcy of life. We all have crossed this boundary more than a few times in our lifetime, which is a sense of review of what is to come or has come already. To actually see what has been seen or played out in our subconscious is a vision of sorts, a great way to say, *hey this is something, intuition is and a great way to actually capitalize on many great thoughts of oneself.* "Déjà vu," if you will, is a part of perceiving in dreams; it's not an actual dream but part of a sequence that is establishing something that will show you have discovered this once before. It's like you have walked these grounds before but keeps one wondering, *where and how?* A flashback of sorts, to part of a dream in the sequence of events that have taken place in a whole picture.

Q. Soul mates, how do we determine who is our soul mate and do we really have soul mates?

A. Soul mates, as it sounds, are from the soul to the soul. This is a job in process, a never-ending work. It's when one is finally at a place of happiness in life with both themselves and their mate that they can actually say we share common ground always. It's also when everything about us has come from such a long journey of hard love and work that created this relationship. We then begin to see the word *soul mate*. It doesn't come easy and nothing in life is for that matter, so for soul mates it's the same. In reality, it takes two and in order to actually steer clear of fantasy issues we tend to look at the hardcore reality of soul mate. Remember nothing in life is easy and especially when dealing with the soul, and soul mates is a great part of that statement!

Q. Do we come here alone to this life and do we die alone?

A. We are surrounded by the everlasting light of *God*. The main thing is this: we never leave Him or He leaves us. Our souls are united over there with many family members from many lives and many different times. We all journey here from the other side with grace among us from our loved ones there who see us off. It may seem like a long time to be here in this life but it actually is only a blink of an eye before we are back home once more. Our hopes and desires of family to be around us happen right at birth in this life and they surround us throughout our lives here. When time comes for us to travel back home from this life as we know it to life on the other side we are guided back home and helped on the other side from family members and angels and the spirit of God. So in essence we are never alone and we always are cared for.

Q. If all people worship in church of God, then why don't they believe in spirituality or in spirit? It all seems the same to me.

A. Hypocrisy has many faces in this life and we all fall prey to it whether you're a devoted churchgoer or not. We are taught that spirit resides in us and we are of spirit, so to me spirituality is much more than being told what is right and right of us, for God gave each and every one of us the right to choose and believe. Faith and the boundaries of faith stem from spirit and God. Therefore we are of spirit and spirituality of the sense where we can actually contact or at best harmonize with the other side is very much feasible in every meaning of the word. In many churches or faiths we are taught it's ok to openly say hi to our loved ones and talk to them for they hear us; they are not dead but among the living. The other side is very much alive and fruitful, and we have envisioned the other side as it has been taught from scriptures passed down for thousands of years. Now take what I have just said and analyze it and you will see if we are taught about the other side and that our loved ones walk among the living over there. Well see it is true. Therefore spirituality is of what I and other messengers who speak of the light of God truly try to display and relay. Those who tend to shy away from this or cover it up by sweeping the truth under the rug, what purpose do they serve themselves or others in the light of hypocrites? Hypocrisy and, let's say, "church teachings" are a very rude mix. We can't misguide our brothers and sisters but only shed light on a never-ending path towards true peace and understanding of the other side. Regardless of what faith or denomination you may be, the teachings from your temple, church, synagogue or where you pray is but a leading hand to show you, guiding you, what lies in "your heart of hearts, your soul." Reflect what is truly etched with the thumbprint of spirit and God and believe!

Q. I have a family member who just doesn't understand and openly states he hates my spirituality…yet I am so happy with my life and the love of God and spirit. Why is he like this or why do people get this way?

A. Deep down people who are like this are actually those who are miserable or in an envious way that it eats them up to see another so happy inside. The fear of not knowing or accepting keeps anyone at bay with anything in life. Envy is the brother of pride and both will end up destroying one's spirit, or at best, putting a big damper on the relationship they seek with God and spirit. Building barriers or walls are hard to break down but never impossible, but to those it seems worthless to see another so content in the light of spirit for they inside yearn for that very truth. Acceptance is a hard virtue for some who don't wish to fully understand the purpose of all; this leaves a void in their lives that is hard to fill for a time period, which gives a shortness of belief. In the end and saying this, *everyone will and eventually do, reach out and seek that everlasting spiritual side.*

Q. Do I have guides and angels?

A. Yes, we all come to this life with our guides and angels; we are set apart from them in our vision and some do see their very own from time to time but they are there for us and with us. During the course of our lifetime we seek guidance and ask ourselves to make the right choices seeking that personal path to growth. There are many times in one's life we feel or even see our guides. This gives revelation to the fact we are here for a purpose to grow in spirituality, learning many lessons throughout life. Our protectors, if you will, the angels are by our sides, and yes, there are times in which divine intervention has happened in our lives; this is a grand way to actually say, *God loves us to send angels from heaven as bodyguards.*

Q. Why don't my relatives come from the other side when I call them?

A. The other side is as here but let's say much more busier in life with so much to offer in harmony and understanding. Realize this: if you were at home busy working away, I called you up on the phone demanding you come at once just for a visit, are you going to drop what you're doing to jump over to sit and chit chat? See the other side is not a place where our loved ones go and sit around eating cloud bonbons all day long. It's a busy place, and remember this too in regards to you, they are making a home for welcoming you when your time comes. People are busy there doing learning as well the teaching aspects of spirituality, comforting others as they too make transition both back home and to here. There is a lot of love sent from the other side even in our time of need; doesn't mean they are ignoring us by any chance. We are really well cared for and loved unconditionally.

Q. Is Heaven real? If so, how do you know for sure?

A. That burning in your gut and in your heart, it makes one desire something bigger than we can imagine. Yearning of home is placed in the road map etched in our heart of hearts, our souls. It is a bugging of the wanting to know, the quest of knowledge, the search of spirit and it all exudes from every thought you have of home. You know that missing or longing feeling you have when you often think of heaven? *You picture a beautiful place in your mindset, yet the hunger grows so deep within.* You know very well there is more and also something of a reflection of sorts. You cascade your thoughts towards the most spiritual place one can fathom and it brings pleasure to you inner soul, giving you the feeling of *right* and it is yours to have. Faith builds character, hope initiates understanding, and longing drives the spiritual essence deep within, thus sharing with you the insight of Heaven.

Q. Are ghosts and spirits the same?

A. In an essence yes but on the same level no. Ghosts are trapped spirits here in this life that have been displaced either by not accepting to go home or feel they are actually in their space and we are the invaders. Sometimes ghosts have been dealt a passing that is so fast or traumatizing they do not accept the rite of passage and linger in this world thinking they are home. It's a real jam to be in for them stuck between lives, but with gentle guidance from us when detected, there are able to reach home properly with love and understanding. Spirits that visit us from the other side are ones that have actually crossed over to the light and accepted the rite to passage. They cannot harm you or would care to. These spirits are ones that come to check up on us and keep tabs, if you will, like family members and such. Spirits that have crossed over will only be loving and caring for us, bringing total compassion and understanding. This is the difference between the two.

Q. How can I enhance my abilities to sense or achieve intuition? A.

Acceptance is the key here; it brings a lot with it once you are the willing of spirit. Acceptance gives a perspective that you are totally given yourself to God and spirit. Assuming you are in good faith and show that the willingness of you lies within your heart not just some whimsical moment of relief to find out the difference.

Meditation helps one to relax and achieve the mindset to actually try and focus on spiritualism becoming one with the universe and all good. Keeping a record of such as well is a grand teacher of sorts, for we reflect back at our achievements to see how far along we have come. Always keep an open heart, an open mind, while accepting what is right and your right by spirit from God. Love unconditionally everything in life for it's from the basis of life we draw strength from. These are the aspects of becoming more in tune with spirituality.

Q. How do I incorporate my personal religion beliefs with my psychic beliefs?

A. Is it not true we hold the temple for the Holy Spirit? God is within us, we are made from him, and we are among spirit for spirit is among us. Spirituality is a great part of religions, for it is in spirit we believe. Having faith in spirituality is as much a part of religion as the sun and rain is a part of this life. It's only those who wish to shelter the two apart from one another that are actually the blind leading the blind. I ask you this: In many religions they speak of many different individuals long ago that have had sightings of spirit as well as communication with the dead. Does that make them the castaways or black sheep of the community? No. It is your right as a child of God that spirituality belongs to you and in you. Fear not what is right or your *right* only fear those who disbelieve for it's them that need the reassurance of unconditional understanding, not some condition set upon the children of God.

Q. Are visions I have during my meditation the same as messages in my dreams?

A. Messages in your meditation come from guides or family members or a higher being that is addressing thought you wish attended too. These visions or messages are set apart from messages from your dreams, for those are your inner self communicating back with you to address certain points of interest. Meditation is a place of relaxation that one goes to seek refuge or peace within oneself. We achieve the answers for things or visions, if you will, to bring a better understanding and harmony with all in the universe. Dreams are personal messages that are received from your inner self, which in turn tells you what is the proper way to address issues of importance surrounding your life as it is.

Q. Can my love hold back a loved one from crossing over to the other side?

A. Love is a tie between individuals with great bond and caring; it is not a nail that holds down another from progression in life here or there. Never at any point should one think that love for any circumstance holds another back from the rite of passage to the other side. Love is the essence from which all greatness grows. It is but a seed that springs forth nurturing and developing within your soul. There is nothing that can hold back a loved one ever, but there is the absolute of disbelief that can hold you back from growing in spirituality; thus you create your own ball and chain aspect of holding someone back.

All in all every question posed over the years are of great value and have great purpose for everyone involved. It's a great thing to review such questions and answers as you have just read here and it gives some type of balance in the essence of knowing and growing. For if we never ask anything what type of society are we? We need to keep our eyes and ears open and a clear mind to all and everything in life for it is in us to seek the right path in any event. Our hearts cry out for knowledge and we crave the inner teachings of God and of Spirit; it gives the foundation upon which all good comes. Life is a delicate treasure of many beautiful avenues to wonder but to actually see the path in which you desire and acquire that knowledge to do well is in you and your heart of hearts…your soul.

These are among a great way of expression for spirituality over the years of questioning one's faith. One can see this only makes an individual grow deeper in spirituality, thus giving the essence of love and compassion for everything they feel toward God. It has been a real pleasure answering all these questions; it gives great insight into spirit and into one's heart where the fires of everlasting burn. The world is changing and at best changing forward for the better as we see in many of these questions.

God bless those who asked for it is your right to seek the truth and understanding of insight of spirit and God. I might not have all the answers to everything but what I have is given freely from spirit so in the light of everyone I share with you the knowledge of what I know. *They say it takes but a village to raise a child; this too holds true to the fact it takes many to walk the path of right to achieve what is right.*

Chapter Eight

Meditation and Relaxation

Meditation is a relaxing way in which one's mind and soul are united throughout a procedure that involves taking your attention away from reality bringing forth a mindset that will enable one to grow in spirit feeling fulfilled. To allow your body and soul to become one in essence is the way we all do every day in little brief moments. Sometimes we are not even aware of it during a course of the day's events. It does relax the body taking away from burden for a solitary moment, which allows reflection for that encounter of peace with you. There is no wrong way to meditate; all it requires is your patience and time. The more we become self-disciplined in this area the more relaxed and willing is the mind and soul!

Meditation is another way of a relaxation technique used to bring your awareness to a heightened level. When you meditate you are bringing your mind, body and spirit to a place where you become one with your surroundings and thought. This enables one's mindset to develop and approach to intuition to a higher respect and gives the advantage of not being so apprehensive in the realm of spiritualism, teaching us patience and many virtues. To release all the day's inhibitions and releasing the negative energies to the universe, offering up the ill will of many problematic situations to God, you are accepting the fact of realization between you and spirit. Becoming whole, as I call it, *is one step closer to the realism in spiritualism*; this is accomplished through the transition of meditation to becoming aware of your inner self.

Patience in spiritualism or anything for that matter is a great character builder in individuals that gives great perspective in the long run. The old saying goes, *in order to be a good teacher first one must be a good listener*; this stands true to meditation as well. Listening to your inner self and the feelings of spirit, everything that we are as spiritual beings gives us an advantage. This advantage will enable us to be more dominate in spiritualism. All through our lives, believe it or not, we meditate many times! This is carried out in many forms that enable us to escape the reality of life in this pretense to find a happy medium within us. You may ask, *what is this, how would I know where to start with this concept of meditation?* Well during our course of our lives we all have taken time to escape the hassles of the day by imagination. That's right imagination is a great tool of meditation. When our daydreams come into play and we slip off in a realm of desired fantasy or far from the activity of the day, we have just created a solid ground of meditative resolve for our inner selves. This enables us to have that one to two minutes' peace, out of body experience if you will of a certain type. No one ever gets hurt in meditation or do they lose any ability of anything whatsoever. It is one of the most exciting ways to recover or even start up the rejuvenation process of our bodies by slipping off to distant land or a thought of far off adventure.

Daydreaming is very useful in many ways; this allows each of us the opportunity to contrast our day, beginning with a refreshed mindset to look at things in a different view at times. Imagine you're sitting glancing out your window, for that brief moment you slip away to a time in your life. This is called reflection and is also a great tool for meditation. Reflecting upon many different times in one's life gives the time for healing or even a time for resolve for we are actually investigating our inner self and the ability to be able to meditate. Whatever occupies your mindset that takes you away from the then and now is evidently meditation at its best! It doesn't hurt, it causes no pain, it's free, that's right free, free is the term used in meditation to be able to be unattached. Becoming unattached to your real life situations, collaborating with spirit or becoming one with the universe, feeling your way through all the practical episodes of meditation is a perfect harmonious feeling. Never give it second thoughts, as I always say don't second guess, for nothing you do is wrong in meditation; it's a road well-traveled. A paved educational trek that many have been through to seek the solace in life, bringing that ever craved oneness with the universe and spirit a bit closer to the soul.

Never underestimate your abilities at any time during your life for you have tried them out numerous times before. This is just a refresher course if you will. Children alone can state what goes on in their daydreams and express themselves freely without any guilt of a desire for more. This is a free will built-in reservoir of spiritual tools we all have; it's the finding them again to become that child once more befriending its true meaning. Now while we have discussed the daydream aspect of meditation, I bet many of you who read this would agree right off having no second thought about it. Some of you will think a bit then realize it's true. Then there are some who need to be shown, for they have actually shut themselves off to the perspective ways of learning to listen to oneself. Regaining that, which is an institutional aspect of meditation, is not only like riding a bike but it actually sits waiting for you to say a fond hello where have you been!

Acceptance is a big word and you have heard it throughout this book, in fact a chapter that is dedicated to the purpose of realization...acceptance! Breaking down the barriers of meditation is not hard whatsoever; it deals with the easiest love of all, you! We all have the time of the day to listen to the radio or watch television, which enables us to use our imagination at times; this is another way to actually escape drawing ourselves in tune with the perspective of meditation. How can watching television or listening to the radio be a meditative aspect? Well it is for if it takes your mindset off the then and now and makes you drift off in a place of peace giving you that solid moment alone in your space then it's a form of meditation. Grasping the concept of meditation is not a rocket science; it involves no real brainpower only power of the spirit that enables your mind and body to become one.

Whenever one begins their epilogue of different spiritual studies, I always say keep a record of it for this is you and your solitude. Keeping a record of your meditative ways styles or habits, let's say, gives you the directive to be able to determine what best suites you. You can briefly look over your notes, which this gives you that extra edge of support by reinforcing the last meditation of spiritualism you encounter. Keeping record will also tell you the progress in the area that best gives your inner self, your soul, the right initiative to grow in a direction of intuitiveness, the awareness of all. Whatever you encounter during your meditation or whomever, whatever the situation might be, record all aspects of your journey. The record serves as a positive move in your enlightenment and growth in spiritualism.

Before we begin, try to find a quiet spot in your home for yourself to relax in, away from distractions and noise. You may want to sit or lie down; it's your choice. Both are very good ways to start off. Once you have found the ideal position you're comfortable with, we will begin to get acquainted with your surroundings and begin to take time for you. This may take a few times before you're very at ease with the idea of meditation but the more you do meditate the better it becomes and easier for you. Try a few relaxation exercises, first by loosening up your body to become fully focused on your journey that's about to begin. It is a most exciting part of your life to regain the ability to freely slip off to a different state of mind, being in full control of and aware of your surroundings. This is as natural and nothing out of the ordinary for meditating. Creating a peaceful state of relaxation is the evolution of both mind and soul. Everything in life needs time to rejuvenate, becoming one, and releasing negative energies. Meditation is a form of relaxation that brings positive-ness

142

from within. When I state reach from within to many, what I am stressing is to find that corner that lies in your heart that enables your soul to find peace, bringing it forward to blend with life in the present. Accomplishment of this gives great satisfaction, which will show you the path that exudes all pureness of both worlds. We hinge our thoughts on a purpose to draw conclusions from meditation to form a conclusion to thought, which gives the total purpose of solidity as one the unification of body, mind and spirit.

You can actually get someone to read this to you slowly in a slow manner, enabling you to relax concentrating on bringing the heightened awareness of you to the forefront. While you begin your journey remember that you are safe while in control. Be not afraid, for this is a great time for you to capture the peace of your inner soul. Well with all this said let's begin your journey among many. May this be a joyous and memorable experience...God bless you!

Meditation

While you lie in a comfortable position or a sitting position we begin with your breathing. Place your hands on your chest if you are lying down; feel the motion of your chest rise and fall. Begin breathing in through your nose, filling your lungs with positive air, thinking positive things that make you happy. We exhale through the mouth ever so opened as we push the negativity of the day away. Breathe in through the nose slowly filling your lungs of the air around you, thinking positive things throughout your life. Breathe out releasing all the tension of the day, as you breathe out let go of the negative-ness. You continue to breathe in and out slowly, filling your lungs full of the greatness and wonder of spirit bringing positive thinking to you. You release the negative feelings that have built over the day, pushing them out slowly through the mouth.

As you are becoming aware of the breathing we start to breathe slower now, in through the nose, out through the mouth. Now I want you to feel your toes as you sit or lie in your comfortable position; feel the warmth of love cover your toes and your feet, making them warm with relaxation. Feel this warmth take over your feet, making them relaxed as you continue to breathe slowly in and out, in through the nose out through the mouth. As you are lying there feeling this warmth on your lower extremities, also feel your chest rise then fall slowly as we go through this process. Your breathing should be very slow at this point, getting slower the more you relax in your meditation.

Feel the warmth coming up your calf muscles, the back of your lower legs, feel the intensity of warmth that cradles you, making you feel very relaxed while you breathe in and out slowly. Your toes and your lower legs are becoming entirely relaxed, enabling you to actually feel very light in that area; concentrate on those areas as the chest rises and gently falls. At this point we are going to introduce a break in your breathing, in through the nose slowly for count of five, hold for count five, then releasing it slowly for the count of five. Let the warm feeling now slowly come up the upper legs; feel it as it goes to your knees, passing your knees to you upper legs, all the while still totally comfortable, relaxed and aware of your surroundings. Your breathing making your chest rise up slowly as you fill your lungs with the positive-ness of energy, then holding for count of five, releasing negative-ness through your mouth slowly for count of five.

Your legs are becoming increasingly relaxed, feeling lighter and lighter as we continue to feel our chest rise with every positive breath in, falling with every negative breath out, releasing the day's tensions and distractions. The warmth of your legs now are going up your buttocks, to your hip area, through your groin area, all the time concentrating on the relaxation of your legs becoming lighter and lighter. Feel the warmth from your hips on downward. As it relaxes your lower body, the lightness creates a nice feeling with every breath in of positive thinking then releasing with the entire negative out of your mouth. Breathe in slowly through your nose for count of five, hold for count of five, releasing it through your mouth for count of five. All this time you're still feeling the warmth that surrounds your lower body, which is now making its way to the small of your back area. Your chest rises ever so gently with each breath in, then collapses ever so slowly with every breath out, while you feel this with your hands placed on your chest.

Your lower back area is now becoming very warm as well, feeling very relaxed and content with your breathing; your legs are very light, all the while being very aware of your surroundings. We are now moving up your back area to release the tension, feel the gentle warmth take over relaxing you even more now. Feeling like a thousand hands are ever so gently warming your back making you very at ease. Continue to concentrate on the breathing, in through your nose for the count of five, holding for the count of five, releasing for the count of five. You are now becoming much more slower in your breathing, very much in control, very much more relaxed. The warmth is now engulfing your shoulders, neck and head area, creating a very light feeling that makes you feel at peace. Let the warmth take over; let it give you that feeling of self-assuredness. The warmth is your friend it will encompass your entire body, relaxing you totally, giving a very gentle feeling of belonging as one.

Reaching out to embrace you is the warmth, which now has moved down over your facial features. As it feels so good, let it run slowly across this area relieving that tightness in your face. Your hands feeling the chest rise on the count of five breathing in, holding for the count of five, then releasing for the count of five. The warmth relaxation that has taken over your body is now becoming lighter, creating a very good feeling of weightlessness. Let this weightlessness become you; enjoy the strange feeling. It is a strange but good feeling to have. The warmth is now passing down your neck area to your chest area; everything is becoming lighter and very agreeable with you as you are becoming weightless. You are still aware of your surroundings to what is going on around you making you feel totally safe. Continue to breathe slower and slower controlling each breath; this is becoming very easy for you now as your chest rises with each positive thought falling with the release of negativity.

You are now feeling very comfortable at this stage of your meditation, becoming more induced into a great state of relaxation. Your body is now becoming much more introduced into the realm of being aware of one with mind and soul, which is going to enable you to do deeper meditation now. Continue your breathing, in very slowly for the count of five, feeling your chest rise, holding for the count of five, and releasing for the count of five the negative-ness through your mouth. At this point your breathing is much more slower now than what we first started out at, giving the relaxation feeling through our your entire body at every breath in and every breath out. If you are more comfortable now to continue breathing through your nose only or your mouth only at this point it is perfectly all right. Meditation is a relaxing mode at which you must feel very comfortable with your abilities and your desires.

I want you to now continue to breathe ever so slowly, feeling your body increasingly becoming weightless. All thoughts are disappearing giving you a complete break from tensions and negativity. Place yourself now in a happy picture, a place to escape too, and your favorite hideaway. Use your imagination to create a secret window of escape, a beautiful sanctuary that is engulfing you and exuding such solace to your soul. Feel the surroundings with your mindset, giving you the pleasure of peace all around you. Let it in your heart, make it a part of you, love every moment of your sanctuary. Continue to breathe ever so slowly, in for the count of five, releasing for the count of five, totally relaxed and in control. This place you are in is very harmonious, alive with spirit. You feel it; the power of it runs through your body giving way to all that is good. Now picture a small running of water; feel the mist as it comes off the rocks nearby. Hear the gentle trickle of the water as it cascades over the rocks; this is giving you the most wonderful sight you could see. The air is so fresh, as you breathe in slowly. Take in that freshness, absorb it, relaxing your mind and body. It's such a solitary place, peaceful, and you're safe with nothing to worry about. Enjoy the surroundings that begin to fill in the landscape around you. Look around see the beauty that is transpiring through the eclipse of trees, flowers, the total essence of love lies within your surroundings. Your sanctuary is becoming much more a safe haven for you; it's a place you can come to any time to escape. The trees are full of leaves, the flowers have such sweet smells coming from them, and the lush green vegetation that surrounds the entire area is so heavenly.

Your so much at peace here; it is becoming of you and you of it. The refreshing sounds start to fill the air now. Stretch out hearing the water as it travels over the rocks ever so gently. The brightness of colors that make the array of a rainbow that breaks over the water's edge enlightens you even more. You're continuing to breathe ever so slowly, deeply for the count of five in with positive-ness of the sanctuary you are engulfed in, gently breathing out releasing the negative-ness to the universe you have created all around you. At this point you decide to pick a flower's scent. Narrowing it down begin to imagine that smell. Let it fill your lungs of its aroma. The sweetness of its textured petals fills the air. You're totally relaxed and loving every moment of this solitude you have created, for its magnificent reverence is now all about you. Listen for certain sounds, the gentle breeze that makes the leaves move ever so slowly in the trees. It's so nice and warm here. You're surrounded by warmth; it cradles you like a newborn baby. Everything becomes more focused for you now, a finer beginning that gives purpose to your oneness with spirit. You feel so much alive with everything around you; life thrives in everything you see, hear, and feel in your sanctuary. Begin to tell yourself to listen for guidance from the spirit within you. Begin to search for a point at which you can feel most comfortable. You're totally relaxed and still breathing slowly, comfortably giving your body along with your soul a chance to join and become one with everything around you.

Start to imagine now your sanctuary growing as you are growing within your heart. See much more peace developing all around you become focused on everything you see. Enjoy the most reverent feeling you can muster, for it is in you to be able to celebrate. Now picture a very white light; it is coming towards you which will surround your entire body, as you are totally safe in your sanctuary. The light becomes bigger and brighter all around you, giving you a peace you feel so dear to you. Reach out, accept this light, and embrace the white light of the Holy Spirit. Feel very much at home here for it resides in your heart of hearts, your soul. You are still very warm while content breathing very comfortably, much aware of all around you. Let the white light surround you completely; feel the love that comes from this. The unconditional love of spirit, the compassion, the truth that lies within you, everything around you is now all becoming as one. Feel free to search your soul asking for guidance; don't be afraid for this is a place of peace and understanding. If you wish to ask for help in any way or ask for a loved one to help you, don't hesitate. This is again a place at which you have created for peace from within. You can stay as long as you wish here enjoying everything that has become you and all around you giving that solace you deserve.

After spending a little time feeling so comfortable it is time to transcend coming out of meditation when you feel it's right. You're still breathing comfortably, feeling safe; we start to back track now. The light, the white light begins to grow smaller now and less intense. You're still very warm and content, very happy. The white light of the Holy Spirit is now moving slowly away from you while you are at your sanctuary, a beautiful place you have created. You feel the mist once again from the gentleness of the water cascading over the rocks beside you. You hear the breeze as it gingerly crosses each leaf in the trees. The beautiful bouquet of flowers, the array of colors and scents they give off are just magnificent. The sights you have painted over the landscape are still going to be here when you return later on as well. Everything you have created in this sanctuary is yours. It's your little secret place to escape. All the beauty it holds, it holds for you in your heart. The oneness you have felt is where you will return many times for this place is now a place of yours and your souls.

We begin to come out of our meditation now by releasing the beauty of the surrounding sanctuary back to the universe from which you have created it. You feel your breathing once more as your chest rises up with each breath taken in while falling with every breath released out. Your body is now becoming more aware of itself as you start to feel the movement in your hands and your arms. Move them around a bit, while still comfortable in your position. Start to open your eyes, look around, and move your head from side to side becoming aware of your surroundings. Your body is now feeling the entire warmth from this meditation; it feels totally relaxed, as it should. Lie there a moment, collect your thoughts, realize what you have just done. Enjoy this moment; it is a moment of peace and tranquility, a memory of many beautiful moments during your meditation.

After you are through your meditation you are feeling very comfortable at this point. I would keep a meditation journal handy to write your experiences in. Keep track logging your journeys always, for each time you do, you create a message that is sent in reflection back to your soul. This will also enable you to look back at any messages received from your travel as well. A solid based record of your meditation, how you felt before, during and after is a great way to solve many problems. This gives the insight of you, of all around you, for records are just that, a place to reflect to that you can adjust anything that needs adjusting.

Congratulations on your meditations I hope it was an eventful journey for you. May you be blessed tenfold and share that blessings with others.

Chapter Nine

Psychic Abilities True Forms

From any precognition or any inkling we have that comes from our gut is the proper and most valuable tool we all have that assists us daily. We often disregard any feelings that give us a prerequisite to knowing what might happen before it actually does. Taking our "right" for granted or not paying attention from time to time does lend credence to the fact we are starving humans seeking the spiritual experience. Every essence of us tells us that what we seem to know and feel at times is from our inner self and spiritual in every sense of the word. Intuition is a part of us like the light through the pouring rain!

Empathy

Empathy is a way the ability to sense other emotions and pain. It also can reveal many aspects to future, present and, yes, go as far as past revelations to one's life's experiences. To be able to adhere to one's feelings, to re-examine situations while trying to comply in helping individuals make heads and tails out of moments it's a true testament of an empathetic person.

Empathy has no boundaries; in saying so one can sense another across the room, a block away, from a picture and, yes, even a phone call. Ultra-sensitive to the ability to determine another's feelings, personal happenings, which take the true compassion, love and understanding in most part, is what empathy is.

To be able, not only to sense an individual but to make a determination in the scope of feelings addressing any situation that may arise from anywhere is a very enlightened and in tuned empathic. Each of us have our very own ability factor, if you will. Those who wish to utilize the potential while harnessing the power are easily adaptable to any ability thereafter.

The energy one exudes or harnesses is more than a protective cover, if you will; it enables one to be able to administer proper guidance while experiencing the other individual without keeping the energy sought out by the empathy.

"Empathy" may be classified as a certain type of individual but in essence we are all the equal and created this way so therefore we all obtain the right and privilege of empathy.

Empathy is a pure energy drawn, given freely in the most certain way possible. It is derived in all of us through the true compassion and understanding of free spirit for all. To be classified to anything less is not true. The fact remains we all have the ability; it's just knowing your true inner self, your heart of hearts, your soul. To have passion with commitment towards spirit in life one must obtain through residual growth in every aspect of spirituality true feelings of insight, empathy being a great part of this.

Harmony between the elements, nature and man strengthens all, build that never-ending bridge of spiritual well-being. Empathy or any ability for that matter has no place for self-indulgence of any type; think everything good and much will arise from any form of spiritual feeling.

If one looks at the word itself seeing that empathy is similar to sympathy and from these two words we generate from spirit a great devotion for caring. The compassion is undisputed love for spirit in all of us and what it has for one another is just that, pure and sympathetic towards our fellow man or woman. In essence we assume the role of "Dr. Feel Good," and actually re-invent certain circumstances be it pain or feelings of such that circulate within our souls and us.

We tend to take on the role of the individual we seek out or say the situation seeks us out. Then we feel the sense of all emotional and physical aspects of that person. Some even as much just have to take a fast glimpse at an individual then can sense fast, while others are drawn in slowly having a hard time distinguishing the difference between what is factual and what is guessing. This is a topic in itself, which we will examine through the process of empathy versus sympathy.

The actual event has taken place. At that moment one has consumed while feeling that person's pain, we will call it factual pain as its premise. Some are so perceptive in reaching a fast conclusion in this area that it actually becomes them a physical pain is felt, hence the factual pain. In another area one will describe a pain to another; in that sense they picture the energy of that person, incorporating it into a psychical metamorphism, if you will. Then you have fictional pain but pain nevertheless.

If one reads another, different character traits are brought through. Doesn't it make sense that certain pain features or elements of physical attributes also can cross over? Being read as part of a whole picture you get a total look at a connection from top to bottom, empathy being part of that picture. Physical traits such as headaches, stomach problem, operational procedures, auto accidents and illnesses are all part of the "touchy feely approach" to empathy. We all have this in the stage of ability while others can develop this to a certain degree. Attunement the special key to enlightenment, the so- called "touchy feely approach" on empathy is in us and for sure is adaptable to anyone in any circumstance.

"Sympathy," like "Empathy," is its sister in relation to the feeling or sensing ability of an intuitive individual. We would not be good at empathy if we didn't have sympathy. The devotion to humankind, the caring of individuals is instilled in us. We assume the procedure of caring each time we see or hear of situations that involve empathy through sympathy. We tend to reach out, feel our way through this life if you will, just as sure as the rain.

Some may choose not to have this ability due to the tremendous amount of pressure one obtains from the feeling process, so they wish to block it or rid themselves of this situational happening. Some can't block this; it's natural to feel when one becomes open to the fact of spiritualism taking on the role of visionary; it's part of the complete package. You can to a degree shut it off if one eludes a situation, in essence it becomes blocked, but we as humans demonstrate pain by absorbing pain through many different functional ways. If we are to be a compassionate society and we all have souls regardless, right there we are empathetic towards each other feeling our way through life in a sense. To be overrun by emotional or disturbing situations, feel those as we actually talk or get a feeling for an individual, it's natural and it's an attribute we have that is hard to shut off.

So if one is picking up signals, you're feeling that individual's misery let's say and you want to avoid this what to do…well sometimes we are drawn in faster more easily to some than others, so to walk away or change your approach is one way to deal with it. To change your approach is to actually avoid an individual at that time while they are going through a horrific situation or deal with it helping out in any way you can by talking to them.

I find at most that when I divulge all information about them, I talk to them rather than keep it in. It is a sign of accomplishment and relief as well, because then you're relating to it and releasing it. If one senses and does nothing about it, not only are they creating premise for what if and why didn't I, this will play on you also. You will feel the pain or situation of them for a while. In order to release this one has an opportunity, if you will, to actually confront it dealing with it at that moment. If one doesn't, it plays on your mind; then you're left in that situation again of being stuck. Again always confront something head on and deal with it directly or indirectly through prayer and meditation; this too helps to overcome sympathy and empathy situations.

To be empathetic towards someone is not a bad thing whatsoever; it is the total opposite, which offers a great insight into the world of love and caring through spiritual means. People who are empathetic in a great way are also people who show more compassion and devotional aptitudes towards spirit and human life. It's through that "touchy feely" episodes we all go through and encounter that make us more aware of ourselves and others who are experiencing emotional...physical...stressful situations. Hence empathy and sympathy do go hand in hand in the realm of spirituality. Again it is in us and about us. Now let's take a show of hands to how many of us are like this and are empathetic and sympathetic towards individuals who fall in those categories...every one of us, right!

Now take a look at it this way, a different view of sorts: you're sitting in a room while you are receiving bad vibes, let's say. You tend to just run off and ignore it never giving yourself a chance to confront...seek out...or even try to realize it then every time you do approach a room your insides still feel the same. It's not that someone is throwing curses at you but instead maybe the energy level is a bit too high or you're sensing someone who is in need of assistance. You can do yourself a great favor before entering a room; that is spend 10 minutes aside for you to do a small meditation. While meditating ask the white light of the Holy Spirit to protect you and give you strength to do your day's work, be it helping those in the spirit world or those outside in the community. There are many prayers that will assist those in their quest for inner peace making them able to desire, showing that desire for helping without being harmed in any way that you feel the source of empathy so much.

Again ability and intuitiveness all fall in line with empathetic or any other title we wish to describe ourselves, all profound words that describe an individual who is aware period. We are all energy, full of spirit. It comes by no means as a direct result of trying to enable someone to be disabled in any sense but it happens because once again we are all magnetic fields and we draw energy to us. The ability to be *able* is in every sense the true meaning of feeling.

Clairvoyant Perceiving

Take a peek into someone's life, get a feeling for whom they are or what they have while sensing things around them retrieving a sense of ability. Having the ability to actually grab hold obtain information for them in a grand way in the light of all good and using it in a purposeful way is in us all; this is what clairvoyant means. When one says I see or feel a window by your bedroom that has a crack in it, this crack got there from you shutting the window a bit too hard, so in essence the reader is demonstrating a prelude to clairvoyance. To be able to obtain information give it properly and successfully share is what we all have the ability to do. Helping one see through the eyes of another, finding items or things misplaced is in essence true clairvoyance, a great way to start psychic ability.

Clairvoyance is a key to everyone every day. What we may take for granted and blow off as coincidence to any happening is ability spirituality in a form of seeing. To grow in this area is an everyday occurrence along with patience and dedication one enhances their ability. One should not hold any thought other than that of wanting to grow while learning as we do. If we could all look at our children, listen more closely, one would find the openness a desire they express in compassion for learning; this is giving us a great intercession for spirituality.

Release any inhibitions that distract you in your quest to grow, setting aside any doubt you may have. To be totally honest to yourself and others, finding the truth is the key to success, no hidden agendas, nothing hidden whatsoever, just pure truth the desire to help. To seek guidance is also great; we are here to learn, so to ask for guidance from the other side in every aspect in one's life lends credence to the fact we too can ask for that same guidance in our journey for clairvoyance. If one takes time to reflect or meditate and in doing so don't hesitate during these times to approach asking for guidance seeking out help in a transition for learning to interpret any message coming in.

The concept of images that pop up in your mind, log them, keep track of all your proceedings as a record to you. It's essential to growth not only for your mindset but to be able to reflect back taking notice to the ability. If one actually enhances the ability they tend to be able to address more to the message, the total scope of an interlude of psychic. To be able to see deeper, further while to seek out more essential information is very obtainable by the growth in all of us spiritually. Each time one senses, that is the time to ask for more insight into what we are seeing. There is never a rush or a deadline to obtain information, which is easily obtainable through practice and getting to know spirit. To ask for more information from the spirit world is in essence asking a friend for help. It's a telephone call home, let's say. We do receive help in the manner we will address to the individual we help. At any time never give up hope or think anything less than you're doing your part to help. Trust in everything you seek as in guidance from the other side. Absorb everything as a great tool of experience. The more you seek out help, the more you obtain help for others, the inner soul grows and your recognition of self-guidance towards self-confidence lends credence that your ability for clairvoyance or any ability for that matter is sound.

Perceiving or Visions

Visions or perceiving is also a part of clairvoyant seeing, which enables one to see circumvented events unfold before they do. A déjà vu, if you will, to circumstance that are the happening before they actually happen. A thought of, *I know I saw this somewhere before and I have been here once too effect or feeling that travels within your soul*. These tend to travel a lot in the realm of dreams as well, a subconscious attribute to intuition. Messages are relayed in many fashions to all of us; this is one of the most common of intuitional factors built in us that stems from our inner soul.

When one receives information that one tends not to understand at this juncture from a vision of this type, it is always suggested to keep a logbook, if you will, to acknowledge this for further reference down the road. Keeping records of visions or tall signs of happenings is a proper way to deal with such messages. In doing so you will release any bad feeling associated with it to the universe leaving you to carry on in life. If one tends to become acquainted more frequently with releasing energy to the universe, they alleviate burden from them, thus becoming more apt to recycle or harness good intentions leaving one more apt to indulge once more in the intuition of spirit.

If one receives images or messages best to keep journal for every type of incoming subliminal or visual contact we have; this gives us a great purpose to keep record of events as they unfold and it shows us the value of intuition from spirit. Logging entries of anything you obtain will focus your primary goal on how you do this. Also you will gain a better sense of evaluating any circumstance.

To see into the future, the actual event being played out before you is a scary thought to most but we are all radars or receivers like it or not it happens from time to time. Perceiving or visions are at most a part of everyone's daily life giving the feeling of many questions that travel our mindset to try to compensate the residual effect of not being so. Intuition is a grand prospect we all encounter in our lives many times; we all are able to receive the messages laid out before us transforming them into viable information to use as we progress down the road of perceiving or visions.

Chapter Ten

Karma

Looking over one's shoulders and trying to compromise with deeds that we think we have rendered properly to another yet we see the suffering or infliction of pain of some emotional tribute laid out by us gives us the false sense of hope for a betterment of inner self. Taking heed to our own actions or thoughts before we actually implement them is a much better way to stay the course while starving any attention given by retribution set forth by our own doing. Making long-term goal plans to rid any action of creating our own karma that will dwell in the house of pain when the wrath is unleashed upon us is but the utmost respect we can give ourselves and thus we starve karma!

"What goes around comes around. What is good for the goose is good for the gander. Do unto others as you wish them to do unto you. For every action, there is an equal and opposite reaction. An eye for an eye a tooth for a tooth." These are but some identification markings of wisdom that is passed down through generation to generation, giving perspective of keeping a close eye on how we act in life. To create the premise of a loving environment for all around or within your circle of life, sometimes things seem to at most go well from a day-to-day perspective. Given the moment in crises, if one has absolute ill intentions towards another in thought, it's the passing of judgment that creates that ripple effect that seems to follow right back upon the murky depths from which it came. It becomes a redundant feeling once we pass through a door that has our names on it stating enter here for backlash exists. At times we are our own enemies, for that battlefield in which great plans of deviation were laid seem to release the calling of the unwanted right back at us.

In some countries they have certain names or variations for subsequence bad happenings one of which is called the "bad eye" or "evil eye." The laying of bad intentions on another through thought, or let's say even the envy of another, lends little to the knowledge of most, but when one creates the envy of another making the energy of which flows through the universe a release of negativity, it will surely rear its ugly head back at you in time. The downfall in most part is our own doing, for we set up our own karma-based reality. If one has harboring of bad thoughts of another all you do is create a pitfall of unwanted-ness within your soul, thus bring out the rage in which you subside. In life, if things seem to have the better part of going wrong, it has the underlying of what has been transferred from your will on others, which in turn is actually a book marking of your own ticket for retribution on your very own life. If you ever wonder why things befall you at certain times in life, it's not too hard to comprehend if one reflects to see what exactly we did in an opposite forum for another.

Words spoken are words of work, in that, what we preach to others make sure you listen well to the sermon for it has the resembling of a true story for you. Take heed to those uncanny remarks or anything out of the blue that you intend another to hear or feel, for once written become the etched work of a poet in the making. The work of one, who carries a wall of resentment in the very fabric of life, will see the mortar in which holds every essence of the balance one desires in life crumble and become the decay upon which ill will resides. The meaning of "do unto others as you wish them to do unto you" has a significant meaning and in respect with every law of life. It shines a great purpose and lessons that flows through the annals of reality.

The imbalance we bring upon ourselves usually exudes itself or backdrops an unpleasant scene in which we have an undesirable happening that leaves scars in our souls. Etched markings of a real daunting task it is that gives precedence to "for every action there is an equal and opposite reaction." A proverbial quest to rid oneself of anger by the taunting of another is the exact opposite of what we really keep faith in…spirituality. Hypocritical of the banishment of righteousness leaves a dwelling of a void of pure ugliness within, a long ladder to escape the very essence of any circumstance for that matter. Undermining our very purpose in life is such an easy task but to retain the pure of will while refraining from the negativity takes practice and complete understanding for all. Surmising any situation or any circumstance lending wrongful intention is not the insight from which we are taught. Reach down deep grab that inner light and shed the purposeful love for all. Create the happiness from within; become the never-ending solid wall of compassion for all while releasing all negativity to the universe. Let God carry the burden for that is what he wants. To draw conclusions upon conclusions leads to a dismay or resentment from within; thus we cannot see the forest from the hills because we cut off our noses to spite our faces.

The electrifying absence of malice leaves one whole, which gives proper wholesome virtues for a list of undoubted contributions for all. When one feels on such a high, they travel a road that has been traveled many times before by virtually everyone in life, in turn giving a fabulous glare of what perfection in the heart feels. Decree a reprieve for oneself showing the emotional fortitude to reach out carry nothing more than your heart on your sleeve; this will allow the growth in spirituality to blossom tenfold. Sometimes in life it is best to listen, for every great teacher in order to teach has to listen; your heart promptly displays this in every episode of life. The eyes and ears of you lie within your heart, giving that balance we so require to enable each of us to become the acclaimed renaissance individual we seek. Forego any obstacle that may predicate resentment, anger, hate, and envy for this is nothing more than the whitewash that runs so temptingly through our inner self, leaving nothing but a deep hole of despair. Lavish the loving side of everything in life; become the reprisal for all beauty under everything dark; cascade every part of enlightenment that keeps the torch of everlasting burning bright. Seek what is the *right* of spirituality in you, bringing forth all well-wishing that drove that very essence in your heart.

Subject yourself no more to the torment and the rise of ugliness; push aside the feeble-minded outlook on everything, as you chart a path of paramount new beginnings. Set forth the quest upon your purpose in life seeking only the good will of all. The shallow representation of the darkened recluse to which has buried itself within, vacate its premise and relocate the absolute of all good. The sheer elegance that rides upon the virtue of spirituality does not carry a mask, or does it resemble anything other than rightfulness. The mirrored image of our inner self portrays the meaningful elements in life; trust the intuitional value of you deriving everything from the light of good. Stretch the imagination to the boundaries of what is so simply put, realism in spiritualism...the truth behind every matter that enables one to succeed in proper form.

Advocate your solidarity for spirit showing total commitment for every outcome, which is blessed in your life releasing the negativity to the universe. The temple of the Holy Spirit is in you; it's the altar upon which you praise our Creator, the cornerstones of the epiphany of everlasting truth. I'll intent amongst the crutches of society, which have become the overture for pain in one's life, is easily eradicated through proper venting of wisdom for peace. The accord struck for measures of peace in one's life is accumulated through the distance one goes to forge the alliance with spirit. Circumstantial prelude to anything less is but a martyr's way of merely suggesting cumbersome truth; therefore, failure is imminent. For if we keep it simple and always look forward to better giving's for all, merit has goodness that flows through your heart.

Stay unison with spirit and out of harm's way. Look inward to your soul capturing the ambiance of purity, while always searching among the good in you and others. Tutorial teachings are always a great way of expression but the best-kept secret is the teacher in you as the agenda is to hold class on the pupil in distress who feels the wrong in them. Shed no feelings of wrongful intentions towards nothing in life for this creates a perfect harmony in balance with spirit.

Karma has but a funny way of introducing itself to us all from time to time, and we begrudge the day we lay eyes on it for nothing comes of good when one doesn't give good. My personal thoughts would be this: *do unto others as you wish Karma to do unto you!*

Chapter Eleven

Angels and Guides

Touched by angelic hands or moved by the guidance we so seek, finding the purpose of what is our life's goal and how we go about accomplishing this alone or not alone. The never-ending abundance of love that I feel expresses that through spirituality from which our guides and angels bring forth all goodness that shall follow me in my life. Guide me and protect me through this life to the next letting it be known, I never walked alone!

As a child growing up at an early age I had my angels and guides, if you will, and one would be by my side always; his name was Carmichael. I always referred to him this way growing up to my parents or anyone around. Parents should always become involved in their child's so-called "fantasy...imaginary" friends for this is not a fairytale event. We all can learn much from children for we were children once with the innocence as pure as the white driven snow. Children do have vivid imaginations, so do adults, for as adults we seek the unknown visualizing what it is like on the other side, angels, guides and God. As children they are more adaptable to accept while exuding true feelings of spirituality, for everything good is all they know.

Recording any event for your child over the course of his or her life is an excellent way to express true spiritual content in oneself as well. For learning what comes out the mouth of babes is, in fact, *a true measure of security within oneself knowing only innocence of truth is before us.* Keeping a log or journal as well as talking expressively with your child as they grow is in fact a great way to keep those memories alive with visuals of their guides or angels intact for them. It's never wrong or seemingly upsetting whatsoever to carry on a dialogue to ensure the proper care of a child's lasting memories about family or life in general, so this is true as well for their "imaginary friends." Showing the concern or proper evaluation of a child's life as they grow spiritually is only ensuring the balance for them and yourself capturing the essence of virtue in spirit.

Never discard any information given by your child, for you are only then starting to build a wall of distrust, which is a hard thing to break down later in life. Your child will only wish to speak of what is of interest to them to seek approval in circumstances, therefore when approached on the level of wanting to see your reaction always. Talk about the situation for it will bring much good from it. Never lead them on in the conversation involving the spiritual side, for they will eventually evolve into conversations that will be mind-blowing to say the least. Let the descriptive stories flow remembering to capture them in recorded venues as a logbook or journal to reflect upon at many times in life. Encourage your youngster not to be afraid of anything of spirit, for it is as natural as the rain. Taking part in your child's life offering the nurturing of balance of right and wrong while educating them throughout, is what parents are for. Does it not seem the same to nurture them spiritually for life is all about everything?

Guides

As I have spoken above, Carmichael is my guide and he was very instrumental in my life as a young child. My parents often wondered where I came up with such a name, thinking nothing of it and discarding any notion of spirituality whatsoever. It was hard growing up knowing different thus is why I made mention of how to help your children in such ways it will bring lasting memories for all.

Guides help us all in our daily lives, lending that helping hand of what is right and what is wrong. In our vast lives we lead, we all can use that extra little encouragement or mapped out excellence, if you will, to show us or lend that special directional fortitude we seek. We are helped many times throughout our lives here in this life, which we are so blessed to know we are looked after. Whenever we stumble in life we tend to look for the way out, a resolve to particulars that will leave us all feeling safe once more in our environment of life. Granted we all think appropriately that, *yes I got myself out of that jam once more phew* and move on leaving nothing to award our guides but looking upwards saying thank you.

Taking notice every once in a while to the effect of how we all are just human is where we have the edge guided by spirit to do well in this life. We never travel a road that isn't marked for some destination in life. Thus our guides or "the little man on our shoulder" guides us from time to time giving us that moral judgmental call or the "voice of reason." Taking this into account look back in your life now finding those many attempts at seeking the proper course of action, then seemingly see that you have called upon help many times seeking that resolve that can only be brought through spirit. There are numerous times in one's life we seek help from the other side or from our guides to conquer or quest life's journeys. It's in us that mapped out or etched in our heart of hearts who we are, where we belong, who is actually watching over us; our souls know all this, and in time, little by little, it is shown us to give us purpose in life.

Capturing the very essence of who we are and our purpose in life is a trek in which takes a lifetime of learning, for we are all pupils in this vast school of lessons. In order to be a great teacher in life, to pass it on to our generations, we need to first be a great listener in life and what it offers us. Listening to your inner heart your soul and what it can offer you, while reaching out to your guides finding the comfort zone of a true listener it will leave you captivated by any response you receive. Becoming more aware of your inner self and what is around you, those who are sent to protect you in this life are from the love of spirit. Your guides are here to assist you throughout your life helping you along to make judgmental calls when you ask for guidance, which in turn you always seem to learn a lesson that will stick to your memory forevermore.

When we hear those words that cross our mind's eye that give balance in every approach to a situation to find resolve we have our "voice of reason" right alongside us giving that guidance we so desperately seek. Those times of caution to which we often receive are that of a guide letting us know we might be in a trouble spot, therefore to actually back off. Many times we travel a road less traveled but seem to break new ground in the event of getting by or surviving another day. We never travel alone in this life as far as judgmental calls are for; sure we are free to choose what we will in our vast life but in the end we all ask for the right answers in dealing with situations throughout.

Guides offer us that reflection upon which we all derive subtle or suitable answers for. Whenever you feel yourself in a bind that you can't see the light before the pouring rain, we reach out for help and somehow miracles happen and we say thank you so often for Divine intervention. We are not just merely placed on this earth to wander about aimlessly to fend for ourselves at any point in life, or are we just a creature of circumstance evolved from apes to which we have a mentality now of a human quality. We are much more than that, for we are spiritual beings searching for life's lessons learning while coping with everything that is passed our way throughout this abundant transformation from this life to the next. Guides are our helpers in this life; we choose them as we come here to this life and some are actually, like everyone has known, family members who take care of us. Now you're going to say how would I know this? When we say to one another I love you while you're looking in your mother's eyes, as a child that bond is the strongest bond ever; nothing in life can take it away or in the afterlife. That gut feeling you and everyone has is an intuitional guide of your own, giving you the purpose to know while searching out the truth behind each matter in life. When you ask yourself is she or is he watching over me, chances are one hundred percent they are; therefore you have gained a guide or a personal angel on your side.

We are more than just flesh and blood living in a world of concrete for again we are spiritual individuals who have the vast knowledge etched in our hearts about what life is really about. We all have this and much more. Our guides reinforce us along the way giving us the opportunity to grow in spirit and spirituality finding our way in this life seeking those answers we so desperately need. Never for a moment in time think anything other than, *we are never alone and all those misconceptions of oh you're lucky or you have the luck of the Irish*, the truth of the matter is inside you. Truly understand and know the significance of guides, for ask yourself this question: Why do I look up and ask for help from loved ones, from God, from any angelic spiritual happening whatsoever, seeking guidance to overcome any situation or problem? This is a true testament to the fact we all as humans look for a spiritual resolution to our lives and in doing so seek the guidance of faith, understanding, compassion and the truth.

Our guides offer us a complete package of comprehensive coverage throughout our lives, which entails great fortitude in everything we venture to take or obtain in this life. We seek answers to be able to comfortably live our lives as we learn the lessons we gain from every aspect of what we are. When we are down and in need of comfort to see an end to the misery we have become, our outstretched hand is more than asking for help, it's a friendship alliance between our guides and us to be able to resolve a matter of interest. Giving us the aptitude to decide on our own is what we are, but times call for a nudge of relief at times and we receive it every so often.

Comforted for the day or a huge shoulder to lean on in crises, never disregard your guides for the warmth you feel when you feel spiritual in a moment of circumstance, for it's exactly that of guides coming to your rescue to lend that open hand of love. Accepting the fact we are spiritual beings and opening up our hearts leaves no room for faltering in the thought of *angelic guidance* at all. The amount of care we are given is measured in the amount of love deep inside you that wants to burst out and cascade over everything beautiful giving total purpose to everything in existence. The yearning we all have for home, that burning desire to learn more and accept more, that feeling of belonging that captivates our hearts is giving an everlasting impression of nothing more than the absolute goodness of spirit.

I remember a time my wife was out watching television and I went to bed early that evening. That feeling everyone has when a loved one is near, the sensing of another close by, well I woke up knowing she was coming to bed. I glanced up, looked over and saw her two guides. For a brief moment being caught off guard one becomes freaked at a situation as such. After gathering my thoughts, I saw the two most beautiful angelic guides of hers; they were flowing in golden light one male and one female visual to me. Their hair flowed so gingerly and the clothing they wore was robe like and very angelic indeed. The air was very light; a presence of calm was in the air as I witnessed this unfold before me. I later described to my wife what exactly I was seeing, the angelic wavering of love and calm that filled the air it was but so magical to see and feel. The illumination of what was around my wife took a huge part of me to digest at the time for being woken up from a deep sleep was very eye catching indeed!

My one daughter, Cherish, has often talked to me about her imaginary friend she has, which is a great thing for keeping our children in tune with spirituality. It is the proper way of learning for them. She described her friend to me and said they play dolls, talk about things, which she says the little girl spends a lot of time with her. Mackenzie, my other daughter, has the sense and has seen spirits in the upper part of our house to which she has come down screaming. I know as Mackenzie grows, she will too be like Cherish, having the openness to spirituality and the understanding of the other side. Our guides as children usually come across as, "imaginary friends" or "friendly ghosts," but as we get older we eventually move beyond the fact of this and take the knowledge of "spirit guides."

Angels

From the time we set off on our journey to this life from the life of the other side we are given angels as well to look over us to keep a harmonious safety with us if you will. We are blessed to say the least to have been "assigned" angels to look over us and in saying so if we ever have come across a time of need it would be in a position of harm or distress that we are comforted through "angelic divine intervention." For the most part growing throughout our lives we do come across many instances of becoming involved in mishaps or very close calls to which may have caused us harm in some fashion. When we have intervention on our part and we say, *I count my blessings for getting me out of this mess or out of this situation where I might have been killed let alone been hurt*, you should thank your "angels" for the upper hand.

There are times in my life where I have been so close to either perishing that the intervention of angelic relief was there for me. As I describe in my first book, *A Link to Heaven...Chats with the Other Side*, the explosion that took place and the hands of "angels" set me down without a scratch. I am sure others can relate to as well and I will give another example.

I was going to the store one day for my mother to buy cheese on this certain corner where the storefront was very close to the road. The steps were a mere say five feet from the street corner a quaint little store and they had the best cheese around at that time. While I crossed the street I looked both ways as usual like everyone would do to make sure of one's safety. There wasn't a car in sight, not for a long way down the road. I was but a ten seconds crossing to get to the other side of the street. No sooner I was on the other side of the street, I kind of skipped up the second step of the store front, I heard a loud noise behind me. Normally I don't skip or run up stairs but walk normally. I turned around and by inches there was the front of a vehicle off the road onto the sidewalk inches from the very step I just left. When I examined this thinking, *the feeling I had at the time was what I knew and felt*. I felt like hands grabbed me, lifting me fast up those steps to avoid being struck by this vehicle.

I will never forget that feeling or that day. While looking back at that situation I do know, *angelic intervention* came into place saving me that day. It's situations like this we all can relate to and take heed to, for it's not a matter of luck or a coincidence this happened. I felt those hands once more like the time of that explosion and one tends not to forget that certain feeling ever in their lifetime. It's most certainty that that remains in my heart, knowing what I do as I go through life, reflecting to every situation that has befallen me throughout. A greater sense of well-being, is a surrender of the known, giving the purpose and understanding that angels are our protectors from time to time. This gives you and me the assurance we all seek in this life.

There are times throughout my life as a child, as in everyone's life, angels play a huge role and being able to actually see or have vision of them is not impractical at all. Many of us have had the insight in life to have been able to see angels or been blessed to be touched by an angel; this gives a greater purpose to anyone's life. We receive comfort from our angels in time of distress or in an hour of need, thus we do draw strength to carry on in our lives for another day. Angels play a big role in our lives to which being grateful is never enough! In respect, we are the luckiest individuals alive to have such warmth and compassion given us.

Those intimate moments where we feel so vulnerable to life's expectations and we have recourse to seemingly feel obstructed from our inner self, it's a sign of reaching out, dealing with the absence of a grounded foundation in spiritualism. Our angels protect us in many ways that give us a grand look at who we are in this life we have created. Never underestimate the power of "divine intervention" in any respect, for it's the leaning of that shoulder or laying of the hands upon which we are granted reprieve or solace, for then security and shelter of love we so desire and seek is given us.

Our angels that accompany us to this life are with us from the time we are born to the time we cross over and are protected throughout. We often speak of that, "special angel," which we keep in our pocket tucked away for emergency purposes or the one that sits on our shoulder to keep a watchful eye out for us. Well all these little, "clichés" or "wives tales", which are passed down generation to generation, may not be so funny to look at after all. Many things in life we take for granted or have our own way of expressing the truth may come up through different scenarios, but in the end what is spoken is usually the truth. Keep in mind the angel that sits upon your shoulder is actually the guard of your soul helping you along to grow while achieving what is necessary in this life.

The one in your pocket is the one that constantly saves you from any harm that may be falling your way. The hands that have touched you, giving you the angelic feeling, is the angel of compassion that so loves you. We have many angels that look out for us and when we have a loved one that passes over we say, *I have a special angel that keeps their eye on me.* Well you have just spoken the truth for we are never left on our own for family members are the biggest angels we have in a true fighting force for us.

They never just die and pass on to the other side; we gain an angel on the other side who in turn gives us the nurturing and development we need so desperately in this life. Angels sing out praise, giving us the fortitude within to grow sound in our spiritual trek in this life to the next. Be assured that we never walk alone in this life and take heed to all around you....*your angels are beside you all the way...Amen*

In Conclusion

The love of spirit from God gives every one of us the purpose in this life. This enables all of us to accentuate our innermost feelings to feel our *right* as spiritual beings. Our spiritual quest that we all seek from the time we are brought to this life and to the time we return home be an endless sea of lessons to which we all gain from the road map we so delicately etch in our souls. This book, *Signs from Heaven*, illustrates that vast knowledge of sequential events one takes on a journey throughout his or her life with the guidance of poetry in the form of the four cornerstones, *Truth, Compassion, Understanding and Faith.* You are the pillar upon which God builds his church; you hold the Holy Spirit within the walls of your heart. Everything in life you accomplish is through the betterment of all, the mass of which spirit enlightens the very essence of your existence. I wish all of you who have picked up and read *Signs from Heaven* all the very best in life. May you find the solace in your heart knowing we never walk this plane alone because our loved ones are always with us. Journey a well-traveled road of spirit, for the light at the end of the tunnel is only a new beginning not an end!

God bless you all!

Glossary

bbl–be back later brb–be
right back hb–hurry back
hehehe–laughter or giggle
hmmm–thinking…
lmbo–laughing my butt off
lol–laughing out loud omg–oh
my goodness ty–thank you
tyvm–thank you very much
wb–welcome back
yw–your welcome
(((())))–hugs

Reviews on *Signs from Heaven*

In this day and age, there are many messengers of God, lending help in strengthening our relationship with the human spirit. I was consumed by love so unfathomable, I did not want the book to end. Robbie's words permeated my very existence and were indelibly inscribed in my mind. Thank you Robbie, for having the courage and love to share these messages with all who will read Signs from Heaven. For you are a true "Pillar of Light" a messenger of God!

–May Leilani Schmidt
Achieve Radio Show Host/Spiritual Healer

Also by Robbie Thomas...

A Link to Heaven...Chats with the Other Side
General Store Publishing House Canada
www.gsph.com
1-800-465-6072 or

ALSO CHECK OUT
To You from Spirit

You can also log on to www.robbiethomas.net to check out shows and times Robbie Thomas will be appearing. You can also book your private session with Robbie Thomas through the contact page at his web site.

Made in the USA
San Bernardino, CA
01 April 2014